Famous Dirigibles: The History and Legacy of Ligh[t] the Renaissance to Toda[y]

By Charles River Editors

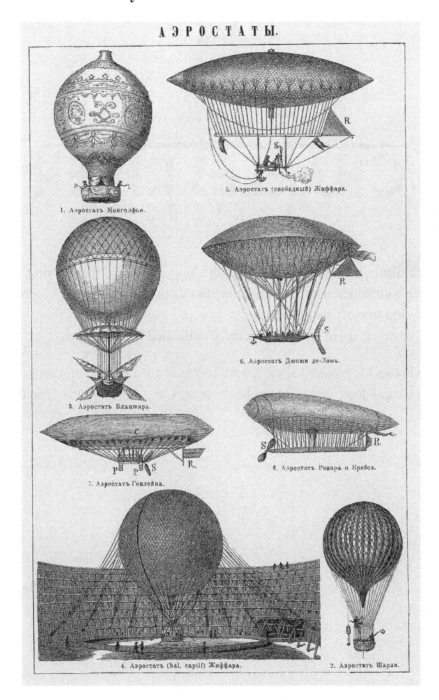

An encyclopedia's illustration of dirigibles before the invention of planes

About Charles River Editors

Charles River Editors is a boutique digital publishing company, specializing in bringing history back to life with educational and engaging books on a wide range of topics. Keep up to date with our new and free offerings with this 5 second sign up on our weekly mailing list, and visit Our Kindle Author Page to see other recently published Kindle titles.

We make these books for you and always want to know our readers' opinions, so we encourage you to leave reviews and look forward to publishing new and exciting titles each week.

Introduction

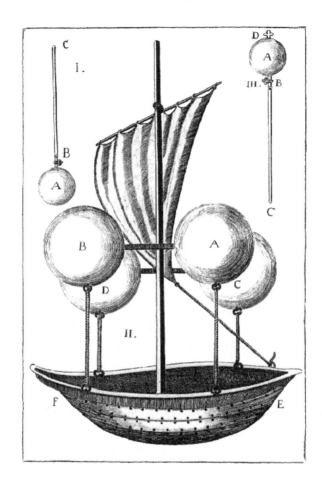

A picture of Francesco Lana de Terzi's design in 1670

The Wright Brothers initially underestimated the difficulties involved in flying, and they were apparently surprised by the fact that so many others were working on solving the "problem of human flight" already. Decades before their own historic plane would end up in the National Air & Space Museum, Wilbur and Orville asked the Smithsonian for reading materials and brushed up on everything from the works of their contemporaries to Leonardo Da Vinci. Undeterred by the work, and the fact that several would-be pioneers died in crashes trying to control gliders, the Wright Brothers tested out gliding at Kitty Hawk in North Carolina for several years, working to perfect pilot control before trying powered flight.

In December 1903, the brothers had done enough scientific work with concepts like lift to help their aeronautical designs, and they had the technical know-how to work with engines. On December 17, the brothers took turns making history's first successful powered flights. The fourth and final flight lasted nearly a minute and covered nearly 900 feet. The Wright Flyer I had just made history, and minutes later it would be permanently damaged after wind gusts tipped it over; it would never fly again.

A decade later, aircraft appeared in the skies over the battlefields of World War I, but they did not represent a complete novelty in warfare either, at least not during the early months of World War I. While airplanes had never before appeared above the field of war, other aerial vehicles had already been in use for decades, and balloons had carried soldiers above the landscape for centuries to provide a high observation point superior to most geological features. The French used a balloon for this purpose at the Battle of Fleurus in 1794, and by the American Civil War, military hydrogen balloons saw frequent use, filled from wagons generating hydrogen from iron filings and sulfuric acid. The balloonist Thaddeus Lowe persuaded President Abraham Lincoln to use the airships for observation, communicating troop movements to the ground with a telegraph wire. Lowe himself reported, "A hawk hovering above a chicken yard could not have caused more commotion than did my balloons when they appeared before Yorktown." (Holmes, 2013, 251). The Confederates agreed with this assessment: "At Yorktown, when almost daily ascensions were made, our camp, batteries, field works and all defenses were plain to the vision of the occupants of the balloons. […] The balloon ascensions excited us more than all the outpost attacks."

Indeed, with advances in dirigible technology, many military thinkers and even aeronautical enthusiasts believed that blimps would remain the chief military aerial asset more or less forever. These men thought airplanes would play a secondary role at best, and that they might even prove a uselessly expensive gimmick soon to fade back into obscurity, leaving the majestic bulk of the dirigible as sole master of the skies. While this obviously did not prove true, dirigibles proved popular in a variety of different ways throughout the 20th century, and they continued to be complements even as airplane technologies rapidly advanced.

Famous Dirigibles: The History and Legacy of Lighter than Air Vehicles from the Renaissance to Today looks at the development of the balloons and airships, and how they were primarily used. Along with pictures depicting important people, places, and events, you will learn about dirigibles like never before.

Early Balloons and Airships: The History and Legacy of Dirigibles Before the Invention of Airplanes

About Charles River Editors

Introduction

Technical Requirements

Understanding balloons and airships does not require much technical knowledge, but a few terms and concepts are important to keep in mind.

Balloons and airships are lighter than air vehicles (LAV) lifted by the differential density of gas contained inside some kind of covering envelope and the air pressure outside. The lifting agents include hot air, hydrogen, and helium. The envelope may be paper, treated silk, or any other substance that can contain the lifting gas, and large airships contain smaller containers of gas with their own envelopes inside a larger envelope. In essence, the envelope acts as a kind of skin, and the lifting gas are the contents.

Aeronauts, their passengers, and equipment would hang under the balloon in a gondola suspended by ropes from the balloon. The gondola was traditionally made of wickerwork. A ballast might be carried and would be fastened around the gondola for fast release; dropping the weight (often sand in a bag) would make the balloon rise. In a hot air balloon, the heat source would be suspended below the balloon and above the gondola. Some balloons had a release cord that could let gas out of the balloon, a procedure that could be used in emergencies to lower altitude or to land.

Large balloons could lift sizable gondolas, which might be little more than baskets that were the size of small cabins. Airships eventually would be lifted by internal ballonets, allowing things undreamed of in balloons, like dining facilities and sleeping cabins actually inside the airship rather than in a gondola.

The lifting capacity of any particular LAV depends on the lifting agent and the size of the envelope. The larger the envelope (which is expressed in terms of cubic feet or cubic meters), the more gas it can hold, and therefore the greater the lifting capacity. A number of factors affect air density, and therefore the lifting capacity of LAVs. These include the ambient air temperature, the altitude of the launch site above sea level, wind strength and weather, humidity, and whether it is day or night. Hydrogen has the most lifting power, followed by helium, and then with much less lifting power, hot air.

A perfect day for launching a balloon would be sunny, relatively dry, and windless. Summer days would have been preferred early because the longer period of daylight allowed more ballooning possibilities. Night flights did not occur for some years, and bad days for an ascent would be any day with strong wind or threatening storms. Lightning potentially endangered hydrogen-filled balloons.

At sea level and 60 degrees Fahrenheit, a thousand cubic feet of air weighs 75 pounds. Fill a balloon with a thousand cubic feet of helium, which weighs 10 pounds, and there are 65 pounds of lift. With a thousand cubic feet of hydrogen, which weighs five pounds, there are 70 pounds of lift. A thousand cubic feet of air heated to 212 degrees Fahrenheit provides 17 pounds of lift (Godfrey 225). A feature of hot air balloons is that the lifting capacity lessens as the air cools, so hot air balloons need a heat source below the balloon that can be used by the aeronaut in flight to continually supply the balloon with hot air.

An additional lifting agent became available as the 19th century advanced. This was coal gas, produced by heating coal to a high temperature in the absence of air. The gas was piped to consumers to burn for lighting and for streetlights. It was inferior to hydrogen in lifting power, but it was a good deal cheaper, and balloonists could obtain it from any city with a gas works. Gas works were increasingly common in the 19th century, and in due time coal or town gas were widely available and commonly used as a convenient and cheaper replacement for hydrogen.

Many of the books and articles that mention coal gas also use the term "town gas." Town gas was piped to city residents to use for lighting, but town gas referred to any manufactured gas sold to residents. Town gas may or may not be coal gas. Both contained a mixture of gases, including methane and hydrogen. Hydrogen, town gas, and coal gas all are highly flammable and were the principal source of danger for balloonists until the age of helium.

There are three kinds of LAVs, defined by rigidity. Non-rigid LAVs do not have any internal or external shaped structure, and the early balloons were non-rigid. They tend to be circular or egg shaped.

Semi-rigid balloons do not have any internal structure, but the envelope may have some rigid external structural elements, and the envelope may be shaped to facilitate better navigation. Semi-rigid airships may be tethered, like the World War II barrage balloons, or they may have power sources such as the engines on blimps.

A rigid airship has the envelope shaped over an internal framework (usually a light metal alloy) and often has a number of internal gas containers, called "balloonets," each with its own envelope. Rigid airships tend to be large, and zeppelins are the best example. Semi-rigid and rigid airships initially used hydrogen, but that has been replaced by nonflammable helium (Stockbridge et al 173).

Non-rigid balloons do not have a power source for directed flight. Balloons are often tethered to cables, and if they are unmanned, they are called "aerostats." Balloon tethers might be ropes or metal cables, but the weight of the cable could add a good deal of weight. Tethers were sometimes attached to a mobile base, such as a railroad engine or a barge, or even a group of soldiers on the ground.

Manned balloons in free flight are largely at the mercy of wind and weather conditions, and there is little control over flight direction other than manipulating weight and gas volume and using what knowledge of prevailing wind directions an aeronaut might possess.. Many balloons carried a form of ballast, such as sand in bags, attached to the side of the gondola. Should the balloon start losing altitude, dropping some of the ballast would lessen the weight, and the balloon would rise. Letting some gas escape from the envelope would make the balloon descend.

The history of balloons up till the late 19th century primarily involved non-rigid balloons, either tethered or in free flight. The lifting agent was hot air, hydrogen, or coal and town gas. Hot air was supplied by some sort of burner located below the balloon envelope, which was usually open at the bottom for the balloon to receive more hot air. This provided the advantage of giving some control over height.

In the 1800s, people who went up in balloons were commonly called balloonists or aeronauts, and the craze that occasionally emerged over balloons was sometimes called balloonomania.

The Beginnings of Ballooning

From its modern beginnings in France in the 1780s, the interest in balloons rapidly spread throughout Europe and across the Atlantic. Indeed, despite the technological limitations in producing hydrogen and in developing durable and effective materials for creating envelopes, balloons became very popular curiosities and entertainments.

The history of balloons actually went back further than the Montgolfier brothers and their competitors in the 1780s. It is possible that small balloons were made from European paper or other materials, using hot air, a thousand years before the Montgolfier brothers' invention. Roger Bacon, the English polymath and Dominican, wrote in the 1200s that the air covered the earth like an ocean, and people could sail on the air. He thought that hollow, thin copper globes could be filled with ethereal air or floating fire, and then they could sail in the air (Nilson and Hartman 279).

The Montgolfier brothers

The history of balloons may go back even further to China, but historians have not been able to determine anything conclusively. It seems likely that the first modern balloons used in recent centuries in China would have arrived with the Europeans, which included the British, French, Germans, Russians, and others. It's quite likely that Chinese inventiveness included balloons, because a thousand or more years ago they had already invented paper, gunpowder, and the compass, but it remains unclear.

In 1670, Father Francesco Lana de Terzi, an Italian Jesuit at the University of Ferrara, proposed a real airship. The ship would have sails and oars suspended from copper spheres (Allaz 11). His concept was evacuating the air from four thin copper spheres, each about 24 feet in diameter, which would then be lighter than air, creating lift for a ship. Terzi even speculated that such a craft would be useful in bombing and reconnaissance. In reality, of course, atmospheric pressure would have crushed the thin copper spheres. It is unknown if this Jesuit read Roger Bacon's musings, but the copper sphere seems too common an element to be a coincidence.

People had long noticed that in a fire, hot air rose and often took sparks up with it. It's not known who might first have conceived that hot air might be contained and be able to lift things, but the first known experiments with hot air balloons were done by a Brazilian man named Bartolomeu Lourenço de Gusmão. He traveled from Brazil to Portugal to attend the University of Coimbra, and while there, he conceived of a way to make small hot air balloons.

Gusmão

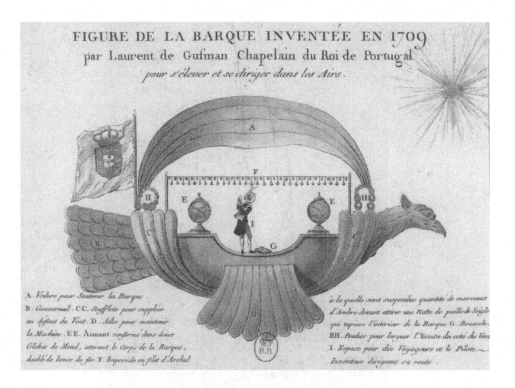

A model design of his airship

On August 8, 1709, in front of Portugal's King Joao V, Gusmão demonstrated the concept with a small paper balloon that rose from the ground and floated around the room. Before the demonstration, he had written the king a letter emphasizing how balloons could greatly increase the speed of sending messages (Allaz 11). The king was apparently entertained but not interested in anything else about balloons. There is no evidence that anything much resulted from his demonstration, which was essentially a parlor trick. In fact, it may have made him somewhat infamous, because he was briefly imprisoned during the Portuguese Inquisition in 1720 for sorcery.

Joseph-Michel and Jacques-Étienne Montgolfier were members of an affluent French family that ran a paper making factory, which allowed them considerable leisure time. At some point, Joseph-Michel thought about sparks and particles rising from a fire and going up a chimney, and he seems to have had a kind of "Eureka" moment. In 1782, he made a small paper balloon, captured hot air in it, and watched it rise to the ceiling.

Eventually, this led to the brothers experimenting with balloons on a larger scale. Starting in December 1782, the brothers began experimenting outdoors. One of their balloons soared up to almost a thousand feet, and from there, the experiments got bolder and the balloons got larger. On June 4, 1783, they gave a public demonstration, with a 35-foot balloon rising to 3,000 feet. This balloon was made of paper with a cloth backing, and the air was heated by straw burned in a brazier below the balloon (Godfrey 228).

A contemporary depiction of the demonstration in June 1783

The Montgolfier brothers were not the only French experimenters with balloons, and hot air was not the only gas to power them. On August 27, 1783, Anne-Jean Robert and Nicolas-Louis Robert launched a 12-foot balloon filled with hydrogen, far more efficient than hot air. They obtained the dangerous hydrogen by pouring sulfuric acid over iron filings. Their balloon, the *Globe*, was released and flew for 45 minutes before landing 15 miles away. The villagers where the balloon landed attacked it with pitchforks and knives, destroying it out of a mistaken belief that the balloon was the Devil's work.

PREM:ER VOYAGE AÉRIEN EXÉCUTÉ DANS UN AÉROSTAT À GAZ HYDROGÈNE
PAR CHARLES ET ROBERT, Le 1ᵉʳ Déc 1783. DÉPART DES TUILERIES.
COLLECTION 476.   1ʳᵉ Série (N.º 5)   ROMANET & Cᵉ IMP. EDIT PARIS.

A depiction of the Robert brothers balloon

In September 1783, the Montgolfiers worked on a large balloon, but it was destroyed by rain. They quickly built another, the *Martial*, which was launched on September 19 from the grounds at Versailles. The launch attracted an estimated 100,000 spectators as the balloon flew for two miles over the course of eight minutes. The passengers aboard this balloon were a sheep, a duck, and a rooster, suspended in a wicker basket under the balloon. During the flight, the sheep kicked and injured the rooster, and by the king's order, the sheep was added to the menagerie at Versailles. The king was pleased with the flight and authorized manned flights (Allaz 10). What happened to the rooster and the duck ultimately was lost to history.

By this point, a rivalry had developed between the Montgolfier and the Robert brothers. The Montgolfiers experimented with some tethered flights, and Francois Pilatre de Rozier was the first human known to fly in an aircraft. He was aboard a tethered Montgolfier balloon on October 15, 1783 (van Eaton 3).

On November 21, 1783, Pilatre and the Marquis d'Arlandes flew 25 miles, but once he became concerned about the danger to an aristocrat's life, the king offered two condemned prisoners for use as guinea pigs. One wonders what the prisoners would have done had they flown 25 miles from the authorities in an unpredictable direction.

Meanwhile, the Robert brothers persisted in their hydrogen balloon experiments. On December 1, one of the brothers and a scientist named J.A.C. Charles launched from the Tuileries gardens in Paris, rising to 2,000 feet and drifting some 30 miles. The balloon was well provided for, with cold chicken and a generous supply of champagne (Holmes 17-18). Robert got out when they landed, while Charles, perhaps motivated by scientific curiosity, got back in and was lifted to about 9,000 feet (Murphy 6). A height of almost two miles was by far the highest any human had ever ascended without climbing a mountain.

A depiction of the December 1 ascent

The first British balloon flight came in September of 1784 and was conducted by the transplanted Italian Vincenzo Lunardi, who traveled from London to Hertfordshire and took along his pet cat as fellow passenger (Holmes 23). It perhaps illustrates British sensibilities that he was criticized for putting his cat in danger.

Naturally, people in London and Paris quickly became fascinated by balloons, a fascination intense enough to give rise to the word "balloonomania." At the same time, there was a lot of speculation about what balloons could actually do. Erasmus Darwin, Charles Darwin's grandfather and a scientist in his own right, believed that a balloon could be attached to a wheelbarrow and allow a laborer to carry very heavy loads of fertilizer up a hill. Scientist Joseph Banks thought that if a Montgolfier balloon was attached to a heavy wagon ordinarily pulled by 10 horses, it might require only a two-horse team.

The fact that such eminent scientists engaged in such mundane speculations shows that it was far from clear what balloons could actually do. For example, Benjamin Franklin, then American ambassador to France, wrote that 5,000 balloons each carrying two soldiers could move 10,000 troops across the English Channel in a single morning (Holmes 19-22).

These early flights were widely covered in correspondence, journals, and newspapers, and an enthusiasm for ballooning that came close to a mania followed. In February 1784, two Italians ascended from Milan. In June of that year, Elisabeth Thible became the first female aeronaut in a balloon launched over Lyons. It is said that Thible sang bits of opera during her flight, which suggests it was designed to get the public's attention. Also in June in the United States. Edward Warren, 13, ascended in a tethered balloon over Baltimore (Murphy 6). Warren's ascent may well have been because, as a boy, he was lighter than a grown man and therefore easier for a balloon to lift.

Balloon launches anywhere sometimes drew very large crowds. The omnipresent potential for disaster must have given it a certain kind of excitement for spectators, something like races today.

Certainly not all ascents in balloons ended happily. There are reports that a balloon with two passengers crash landed in the town of Strasburg. The landing damaged several houses and caused a riot (Nilson and Hartman 291).

A highly significant flight in 1785 was made by Jean Pierre Blanchard and John Jeffries. Jeffries was a Boston-born American, a surgeon in the British Army (Allaz 12), and their flight goal was crossing the English Channel from England to France. When the balloon lost so much altitude it was barely above the water, they had to throw everything overboard, including most of the clothes they were wearing. They even had to urinate over the side in a desperate attempt to lighten the balloon. They barely made it, and the sources are silent on how people reacted to the two nearly naked men climbing out of their gondola as they landed (Pearl).

An earlier attempt at crossing the Channel by pioneering balloonist Pilatre de Rosier and another man had resulted in disaster. Their balloon was a new design, a hybrid of hot air in one compartment and hydrogen in another. The combination was an accident waiting to happen, and it did. The hydrogen caught fire and exploded, killing both men (Balloon Museum).

Balloons were for a considerable length of time popular entertainment, a kind of performance. Launches were widely publicized, often well in advance of the scheduled date, and admission was charged. A few spectators became actual paying passengers, usually in tethered balloons, and the crowds could be rowdy. The ballonomania lasted for several years, even including fashion - some lady's hats were shaped like balloons, and depictions of balloons were featured on such items as clocks, dinnerware, furniture, and even umbrellas and napkins (Pearl). Like the balloons themselves, those balloon hats must have been difficult in a wind.

One related event was the first parachute jump from a balloon. In October of 1797, Andre Jacques Garnerin parachuted from an altitude of 6,000 feet (Smith 146). Parachute jumps had been made before, but to jump out of a balloon in 1797 from over a mile high required being brave or foolhardy.

The First Military Balloons

The military possibilities of balloons were considered early on. Benjamin Franklin, who witnessed some of the balloon ascents, noted that balloons could carry troops across enemy lines and that 1,000 balloons could be built at the cost of one ship of the line (Murphy 7). That could have been a serious consideration, especially since no other nation could afford Britain's scores of ships of the line. Every British rival would have loved to render the Royal Navy useless.

The first military uses of balloons came in 1793, when two French border fortresses were under siege by Austrian forces. In May, General Chancel, commanding the Conde de Escaut fort, wrote a message and sent it by a small balloon. The balloon fell into Austrian hands, and the letter still resides in an Austrian museum. In June, the commander of another fort tried the same method and also had it fall into Austrian hands (Allaz 12-13). Both incidents illustrate how random and essentially uncontrollable balloon flights were.

Even in the midst of the French Revolution's chaos, the French government was interested in balloons. The Committee on Public Safety authorized a chemist, Jean Marie-Joseph Coutelle, to construct some balloons for observation and scouting. Coutelle developed a dozen balloons using a different method of generating hydrogen than pouring acid over iron filings. The process was called the Lavoisier-Meusnier method, and it involved heating tubes filled with metal filings and extracting the hydrogen from steam (Murphy 7-8).

Coutelle

Coutelle's experiments impressed the French leadership enough that the decision was made to authorize a formal balloon company. On April 2, 1794, the French set up the "1er Compagnie d'Aerostiers." The Company consisted of 25 officers and men, uniformed in blue (van Eaton 4). This outfit can claim to be the ancestor of all the world's air forces. The Convention also ordered the creation of a second balloon company and set up a school, Ecole Nationale Aerostatique, to train balloonists. This school is the ancestor of all the world's air force academies.

The Company was quickly involved in military action. At the Battle of Fleuries in 1794, Coutelle and a general named Morelot were aloft observing for 9 hours. They dropped weighted messages by the clever method of enclosing messages in small bags weighted with sand and outfitted with rings so they could slide down the tether cable to the ground. The messages from the observation contributed considerably to French success in the battle (Murphy 8).

A depiction of Coutelle in a balloon at the siege of Mainz

The companies eventually fielded four balloons. Their equipment included horse-drawn vehicles for carrying the balloons, portable hydrogen generators devised by Lavoisier, winches, tether ropes, observation equipment and hanger tents to house the balloons (Holmes 28). French field artillery was the best in the world, and the experience with moving the guns, caissons, and other equipment probably transferred seamlessly to balloon service.

Balloons were involved in a number of battles, including Mainz and Mannheim in 1795 and several more in 1796. Many of the battles were fought during a French invasion of the various German states (Germany did not become a unified nation until 1871), and this was the high-water mark of the first use military campaigns using balloons. The First Company was captured by the Austrians at the 1796 Battle of Wurzburg (Murphy 9).

Coutelle and another balloon company joined Napoleon's expedition to Egypt in 1797, but their equipment was never unloaded from the ships and was destroyed when the British attacked the French fleet at the Battle of Aboukir Bay (Murphy 9). The French troops were isolated in Egypt and eventually surrendered to the combined British and Ottoman forces. Napoleon escaped Britain's grasp by taking a fast frigate home to France and future glory.

Napoleon was not particularly interested in balloons, which is surprising given how astute he was when it came to the military potential of just about every other technology. The two balloon companies were disbanded in 1799 and 1802, making clear that Napoleon's generals preferred cavalry for scouting and reconnaissance.

Balloons were used by other nations in the the Napoleonic Wars. The Danes were interested in a device something like a dirigible to use against British ships intervening in the Baltic, but it never was built. They did use balloons to drop leaflets in Sweden advocating a revolt; Denmark was an ally of Napoleon, and Sweden had become an enemy (Murphy 9). This seems to be the first time that leaflets were dropped from the air as part of a propaganda campaign.

The Early 19th Century

Ballooning obviously lent itself to entrepreneurship. Perhaps the most successful of this type of aeronaut was Andre-Jacques Garnerin, who created events centered on balloons that incorporated many kinds of entertainment. The public loved night launches and by fireworks shows provided from balloons aloft. Garnerin provided such spectacles, and his wife, Jeanne-Genevieve, was part of the team. In 1799, she became the first woman to parachute jump. Garnerin took his balloon show on the road, appearing in London in 1802 during one of the periods of peace (Holmes 29-30).

An early 19th century depiction of Garnerin and his wife

Napoleon was not particularly interested in the military value of balloons, but he was quite certain of the value of spectacle as propaganda. In 1804, he commissioned Garnerin to construct a huge balloon that would be colorfully decorated. A huge crown was to be suspended from the balloon to signify the event: Napoleon's coronation as the Emperor of France. The coronation was quite elaborate and carefully choreographed. The story of this very large balloon is one of the most incredible in the history of balloons or aviation. It was launched from near the cathedral of Notre Dame and appears to have functioned well during the coronation. The symbolism is obscure, but perhaps Napoleon meant it to indicate heaven's favor.

During the event, it got loose, flew south over France, and somehow crossed the Alps into Italy, meaning it must have been an especially sturdy craft. Spotted near Rome the next day, the balloon was deflating near the ground, and in a highly improbable sequence, the symbolic crown dangling from the balloon snagged on a tomb, breaking a piece of it off. The tomb was that of the notorious Roman Emperor Nero, and after snagging off a chunk of Nero's tomb, the balloon seems to have vanished into the Pontine marshes (Holmes 31-32). The Romans probably laughed themselves silly, but they would have done so discreetly given that Rome and much of Italy was under French rule.

Napoleon was not amused by the event, and Garnerin quickly lost favor. Napoleon remained interested as balloons as spectacle, so he replaced Gernerin with Sophie Blanchard, which was also quite unusual. It is unclear how this woman became involved in ballooning. What is clear is that she was determined, intelligent, and a superb balloonist. She met the balloonist Jean-Pierre Blanchard, and she quickly went from being his assistant to becoming his wife. As his health failed, she took on more and more responsibility for what can only be called a balloon business. He died in 1810 of a stroke during a balloon landing, and she did her first solo balloon display in Paris only a few days after his death.

Blanchard

Sophie Blanchard set herself up as a rival to the only other woman in ballooning, Garnerin's niece Lisa. Sophie managed to attract Napoleon's attention, and her balloons became a routine part of various imperial celebrations. The French emperor appointed her as *Aeronaute des Fetes Officielles*, and her signature events consisted of night ascents in a tethered balloon and launching a fireworks display from the balloon.

Sophie's style was deliberately daring. She reduced the size of the gondola to a small silver-colored platform, with sides that only reached her knees. Her balloon was small and made from silk. She adopted a particular style of long white cotton dresses and dressy white hats with feathers (Holmes 33-35). Her approach seemed to be developing a dynamic tension between femininity with the ever-present threat of death.

Despite exploiting the stereotype of women, Blanchard was hardly a helpless woman. She was probably the best balloonist in France, clearly the most popular balloonist, and was a shrewd businesswoman as well. In 1811, she went to Italy and was successful in displays featuring the full course of the symbols of Napoleonic rule. Among other things, she flew from Rome to Naples. On one overnight flight, her balloon rose to 12,000 feet.

After Napoleon's fall, the French brought back a new king from the old dynasty, King Louis XVIII, and Blanchard attracted his attention with a spectacular flight and fireworks show welcoming him to Paris. Louis appointed her Official Aeronaut of the Restoration. This might have been intended as humor, but it assisted her career. For several years her night flights with fireworks became a kind of Paris fixture. Alas, in July 1819, the hydrogen in her balloon caught fire. Her balloon landed on a roof, but she slipped and fell to the street and was killed (Holmes 35-36).

By the 1830s, balloons had become reasonably common, but still unusual enough for the public to find them compelling. People paid to watch balloons launch, particularly in France and Britain. Probably the most famous British aeronaut was Charles Green, who didn't start in the business until he was 40, but still made 526 ascents. Green was a canny businessman, and he had found that coal gas wasn't as good as hydrogen, but still had considerable lift and was much cheaper. A 70,000 cubic foot balloon cost 250 pounds to fill with hydrogen, but only 80 with coal gas. Green then negotiated a contract for coal gas with the London Gas Light and Coke Company. Green conducted balloon ascents at London's Vauxhall Pleasure Gardens for 20 years. His large balloon *Royal Vauxhall* could carry 9 people, so paying customers could rise to several hundred feet in the tethered balloon (Holmes 44).

Green was involved in a significant night flight by balloon. On November 7, 1836, Green, Monck Mason and Robert Hollond, all British, flew in the *Royal Vauxhall*. Mason was an Irish musician and balloon enthusiast, while Hollond was a wealthy MP and the main backer of the flight. The balloon had more cargo that the three passengers. It included 40 pounds of meats, 45 pounds of cooked game and preserves, various liquors, dozens of bottles of champagne, and a portable coffee brewer. This seems to have been quite a lot for what was an 18-hour voyage.

The balloon crossed the English Channel and eventually landed near the small German duchy of Nassau, covering about 500 miles in all (not straight-line distance). At the time this was a distance record, one which stood for a generation. It was broken in 1859 by the American John Wise and three others in the balloon *Atlantic*.

The record flight seems to have reignited an interest in ballooning, which may have been its intended purpose. Even the generous supply of provisions may have been calculated, because it is the kind of detail reporters would pick up on. The cooked game and the champagne would indicate that English gentlemen were involved.

An American balloon sensation was momentarily created in 1844. On April 13, the *New York Sun* announced that a balloon had crossed the Atlantic in a trip lasting three days, from Europe to the United States. The sensational story was a hoax penned by a then little-known American writer named Edgar Allan Poe (Allaz 13).

Meanwhile, interest in the military potential of balloons continued. A welter of revolts broke out all over Europe in 1848, and some rebel cities stubbornly resisted the re-establishment of imperial control. When the Austrians besieged Milan, the Italians sent up small paper Montgolfiers carrying anti-Austrian leaflets that aimed to arouse the countryside (Murphy 10).

An obscure Austrian lieutenant, Franz Uchatius, had an interest in using balloons for something other than observing what the enemy was doing. In 1848, he made an 18-foot diameter balloon from varnished linen and paper, which were inexpensive, and he equipped them with bombs. The bombs had a contact detonator, so they would explode on impact. A time fuse, burning through the rope that suspended the bomb below the balloon, would release the bomb.

Uchatius got a chance to put his theories into practice in Italy, which revolted against Austrian occupation in 1848. One of the rebel cities was Venice, surrounded by shallow water and marshes in ways that made it difficult to reach with artillery fire (Ziegler 750-751). The siege commander asked the lieutenant to allow his weapons to be used on the city, and the Austrians built and armed almost 200 of these balloons, set to be launched from the steamship *Vulkan* (Austria was then not landlocked, possessing naval bases on the Adriatic coast opposite Italy). The attack was aborted by bad weather.

Such an attack also had a built-in technical problem. Balloons launched in numbers from a single point tend to spread out in a fan-like series of directions, effective for about four miles over a large target such as a major city. Beyond that distance, however, they would be ineffective. Balloon attacks like this one were not attempted for decades because the range of artillery increased to well beyond the range that balloons could effectively deliver bombs (Ziegler 751),

The British rejected the idea of using balloons in the Crimean War in the 1850s. The French did use some balloons in the 1859 Italian War, to little avail. By the time the Civil War broke out in America, balloons had been used for military purposes by Denmark, Sweden, Russia, the French in Algeria, and at the Austrian siege of Venice (van Eaton 4).

That said, balloons and ballooning remained primarily an entertainment, and the entertainment spread far beyond Europe. Fanny Calderon de Barca, the Scottish wife of Spain's first ambassador to Mexico, described an attempted balloon launch in Mexico City in 1844. The aeronauts were a Frenchman and his daughter, but the ascent did not happen because of a hole in the balloon (Kuhn 111).

A version of balloonomania had come to Mexico earlier. A traveling French aeronaut named Adolfe Theodore had made a number of ascents in Cuba in 1830-1831, and he was brought to Mexico by General Manuel Barrera. Barrera's intent seems to have been to sponsor a public entertainment and thereby enhance his own prestige. Tickets to the anticipated spectacle were sold, but no flight occurred. The aeronaut was jailed but later allowed to leave the country (Kuhn 14-15).

The first balloon flight in Latin America was in Havana in 1828, made by the British aeronaut Eugene Robertson. Robertson also was invited to Mexico, this time by the Mexican serial caudillo, Antonio Lopez de Santa Anna. Santa Anna knew the value of public relations and had a reputation as a fiery and impulsive man. On February 12, 1835, Robertson successfully launched his balloon, and subsequent flights were encouraged by Santa Anna. Crowds could be sizable and admission was charged (Kuhn 16). The sources are silent on what effect Mexico City's high altitude (over 7,000 feet) might have had on Robertson's balloons.

Balloons in the United States

Ballooning in the United States involved both itinerant European aeronauts and native enthusiasts. In 1854, the highly experienced French aeronaut Eugène Godard brought his suite of five balloons to the U.S., including a large one of 106,000 cubic feet capacity. His company included trapeze artists, parachutists, and female acrobats. This airborne circus visited, among other places, New Orleans, St. Louis, and Cincinnati. Witnessing a launch typically cost 25 cents, and passengers could pay for an ascent in a tethered balloon. Despite the show's public appeal, Godard nearly went bankrupt because of the high cost of replacement equipment (Holmes 74).

Godard

Godard's operation spent a lot of its time in America in Cincinnati. The place at that time was a fast-growing city, and the Midwest was still young and not particularly well-populated. It's not clear why Godard would have settled his balloons there, but the city was on the steamboat route from New Orleans to Pittsburgh, so travel convenience may have been a factor.

The three major American homegrown aeronauts were John Wise, John LaMountain, and professor Thaddeus Lowe. The men knew each other and at times were serious rivals, as Lowe and LaMountain were in the Civil War. Wise made a number of flights in the 1830s in homemade balloons, and even though one of his balloons exploded, he escaped harm. In 1837, he made a deal with the Philadelphia gas works to purchase coal gas for his balloons. His ascents continued through the 1840s into the 1850s (Holmes 77-78).

In 1859, Wise set up a flight that broke Charles Green's 1835 record. The balloon was launched from St. Louis on July 1st with four men aboard: Wise, his assistant and protégé John LaMountain, Oliver Gagen, his main financial backer, and William Hyde, a reporter for a St. Louis newspaper. The newspaper reporter is an important detail, as Wise knew the value of publicity, and it's no coincidence that supplies on board the balloon included a stack of St Louis newspapers. Among the other supplies were various sandwiches, brandy and port, a pail of iced lemonade, and a lifeboat suspended from the gondola (Holmes 79-80).

They flew over Indiana and Ohio, on to Niagara Falls, and then ran into heavy weather over Lake Ontario, barely making it to shore (Allaz 14). The flight really was an epic, officially covering 809 miles, a record distance for balloons that stood until 1910. The launch from St. Louis was deliberate because prevailing winds blowing east made a long voyage more likely.

John Wise had a long and impressive career as an aeronaut. Over several decades, Wise made 462 balloon ascents before he died in an accident in 1879 on his 463rd trip.

Wise

Balloonist and putative professor Lowe designed and built a huge 725,000 cubic foot balloon he named *The City of New York*. Over 200 feet high if it had ever been fully inflated, Lowe exhibited it in New York City, where it attracted large crowds. The craft was so big that it was never fully inflated and never got off the ground (Holmes 89).

The first advocate of American military use of balloons was Colonel John H. Sherbourne, who was in Florida in 1840 fighting against the Seminoles. He thought that by using balloons at night, observers might be able to locate the campfires of the elusive natives, but nothing came of the idea by the time the war ended in 1842.

John Wise advocated using balloons in the Mexican-American War, his idea being to bombard the Mexican port of Vera Cruz (Murphy 10). This gulf port was occupied by the Americans after a sharp engagement and was the starting point for the American army that invaded Mexico and eventually captured Mexico City. Wise continued to advocate the potential of balloons throughout the 1850s.

The principal figure involved in Civil War balloons was Lowe, who had long been involved in balloons and vigorously asserted their value in war. On June 11, 1861, he set up a dramatic demonstration for President Lincoln, during which he ascended in a balloon nearly 1,000 feet over the White House and sent a telegram from the balloon to the president. Lincoln, who frequently admired eccentric technologies, was impressed and let his approval be known. In fact, Lincoln's insistence overcame the Union army's skepticism.

Months before that, on April 20, a balloon flight launched from Cincinnati carried Lowe further than intended, and he landed near Unionville, South Carolina. The flight itself in his balloon *The Enterprise* was far and fast, covering 650 miles in just over nine hours. That was an astounding speed for the day, as it even outpaced railroads (Holmes 92). This was just after the attack on Fort Sumter, and at first Lowe was thought to be a Union spy. He convinced the South Carolinians that he was on an innocent flight (Williams 10). Lowe was widely known as a balloon aeronaut, which probably saved him from prison or worse. Had he been executed as a spy, the Union's use of balloons probably would never have happened.

Lowe in the 1860s

The U.S. Balloon Corps was created in September of 1861 by the Secretary of War, and Lowe was named Chief Aeronaut, but it was officially a civilian position (Williams 11). This created an immediate and ultimately unresolvable issue, as it was not clear whether the balloons and aeronauts were part of the military command structure or contracted employees not subject to military orders. The reputation of balloonists was that balloons were spectacles meant for entertainment, not serious use (Scott 24).

Lowe's balloons were of almost immediate use. He ascended at Falls Church in Virginia in time to see Union troops fleeing from the First Battle of Bull Run. Lowe did not see any pursuit by the victorious Confederates, and his report calmed people down (Williams 11).

The high point of the Union balloon program was the Battle of Fair Oaks in 1862. Some of the ascents were made with telegraph equipment, allowing quick communication between observers and people on the ground. Balloon observations at this time helped the Union during the battle, which was part of George McClellan's Peninsula Campaign, an advance on the Confederate capital of Richmond. General McClellan had moved the Army of the Potomac by boat to the peninsula between the York and James Rivers, but ultimately, the Confederates led by Robert E. Lee compelled the Union army to abandon the campaign. McClellan's reputation was ruined, and the promise of balloon observation suffered because later commanders were much less interested in the technology than McClellan had been. McClellan's enthusiasm for balloons probably tainted their use.

A picture of Lowe ascending at the Battle of Fair Oaks

For their part, the Confederates were seriously concerned about the Union observation balloons. They shot at the balloons to no effect, and no Union balloon was ever shot down, but the Confederates devised methods of deception to mislead balloon observers, such as "Quaker guns," tree trunk segments painted black and positioned to look like artillery from a distance (Murphy 12). Since the balloons often drew Confederate fire, balloons were quite unpopular among the Union troops nearby.

Lowe's balloons were robust, made of double layers of silk coated with varnish and provided with "ascension' ropes. The largest balloons could carry five passengers, and they were better than the usual civilian balloons, but they were still prone to damage to the silk envelope by heavy rain or snow, and wind remained a problem. One balloon lost its tether and flew unmanned from Washington to Delaware. Communication was a problem, as weighted messages dropped from balloons were subject to wind. Signal flags were tried, as were telegraphs (Scott 9).

Lowe created a small fleet of balloons for use along the Potomac. Four were used along that river, and Lowe experimented with aerial artillery spotting. He hired professional draftsmen to sketch landscapes, and visible Confederate forts and encampments. A number of Union officers were passengers in balloons. They included a then-obscure but later famous commander, George Armstrong Custer (Scott 10-13).

Lowe eventually constructed eight balloons, all between 15,000 and 32,000 cubic feet and lofted by hydrogen produced by mobile hydrogen generators devised by Lowe. The observation gondolas must have required brave men, as they were two feet square and two feet deep, not much to grip onto in foul weather. Lowe's field units each had two balloons, two hydrogen gas generators, carts for the balloons, ropes and other equipment, and a field telegraph unit that was sometimes used to communicate from aloft. Each unit was manned by 50 soldiers (Holmes 98).

In good weather, observers were sent up 1,000-2,000 feet, and in bad weather, it might be 500 feet. All the balloons operated on a tether with winches to reel them in, and one that got away made quite a story. This rogue balloon had Lieutenant General Fitz John Porter as a passenger, and by sheer luck he landed safely. Loose balloons were at the whim of any breeze or wind, and the Confederates could have just as easily had a Union general air-mailed to them. It is not known if General Porter flew again.

Porter

Early in the war, balloons were lofted using coal gas from nearby city gas works, but Lowe devised a portable hydrogen generator, using thousands of pounds of metal filings and acid. Needless to say, this equipment was heavy, and one solution was developing a balloon barge (Scott 9). The barge would have worked well because of the many rivers in the region. Union barges with balloons are really the ancestor of the modern aircraft carrier.

The Balloon Corps was dissolved in June 1863. Squabbles among balloonists and hostility by some Union commanders were among the causes, but the root cause was probably the fact that balloons were a logistical problem. At Fort Monroe, balloonist John LaMountain (a rival of Lowe) requested 60 gallons of sulfuric acid and three and a half tons of iron filings, which would produce hydrogen for the balloons (Williams 11). Old-fashioned commanders trusted cavalry as the eyes of the army, and horses required easily obtained hay, not difficult materials like sulfuric acid.

The aeronauts who joined the Union were an eccentric bunch. One of them was John Steiner, an immigrant from Bavaria. It is not known how Steiner became a balloonist, but he was a good one who made ascents from Georgia to Canada, making his living from his exhibitions. He was the first man to cross Lake Ontario in a balloon, and another one of his exploits included jumping out of a balloon over New York City and parachuting down from two miles up. Another included winning an 1858 challenge distance race against the French balloonist Godard, thereby winning a $2,000 bet. The balloons launched from Cincinnati, and Steiner won while covering 200 miles (Hopkins 42-43).

Steiner joined the U.S. Balloon Corps in early 1862, and for some reason, he was ordered to Cairo, Illinois, then to a large Union base for campaigns down the Mississippi. In Cairo, Steiner took charge of a balloon called the *Eagle*. The Army was unenthusiastic, but Steiner somehow persuaded Commodore Foote (commander of the river gunboat flotilla) to provide a barge to operate the balloon from, and he made several observation ascents around Island Number 10, a Confederate fortification that blocked Union advance down river. This is the only known use of an observation balloon in the Western theater of the Civil War (Hopkins 44).

Steiner left the service in December 1862, apparently in a huff over issues of pay. One of his ascents carried a most remarkable passenger, a German military observer known as the Graf von Zeppelin, who later lent his name to the airships he developed. Little is known of Steiner's later life, and he vanished from the pages of history about 1875, but a contemporary newspaper credited him with 315 ascents (Hopkins 44).

An additional problem was that balloonists remained officially civilians under contract with the government. It was not clear if they were subject to military orders, and there was some worry that if captured, they might be treated as spies and possibly executed. It also made for problems in getting paid. Indeed, Lowe eventually resigned over pay issues, as did others (Scott 10).

There were three known Confederate balloons. The first was made with varnished cotton and was a hot-air balloon because the Confederates could not generate hydrogen in the field. The second was the best-known; built in Savannah, it was claimed that patriotic Southern women donated silk dresses to be used in constructing the envelope. In fact, the reality was that a sizable supply of dress silk was found in a warehouse (Holmes 104). The dress silk made for a colorful balloon and for a more colorful legend. It was a gas balloon, using gas obtained in Richmond.

It is not clear if the Confederate balloon actually had any real military value. It was used during the Seven Days Battles in the Peninsula Campaign, and that summer, the balloon, named the *Gazelle,* was sent aloft almost daily using a railroad car. It does appear to have improved the morale of the Richmond population, and for a time the Confederates could counter the sight of Union balloons with one of their own. At least once, balloons from each side were in sight of each other (Holmes 104). The balloon was captured by the Union when the tugboat carrying the equipment ran aground in the James River (Murphy 12).

The third Confederate balloon was the second made from silk dress cloth. It served in Richmond from late 1862 until the summer of 1863, when it escaped its tether and got loose. It was captured by Union troops.

The impact of balloons on the Civil War may be underestimated because of the dissolution of the Balloon Corps in 1863, but balloons were helpful during the Peninsula Campaign, and also at major battles around Fredericksburg and Chancellorsville (Scott 7). Moreover, the history of balloons in the American Civil War was not written until well into the 20th century. Lowe did write a report for Secretary of War Stanton, and he later wrote a memoir, *My Balloons in Peace and War*. Lowe may have embroidered his own contributions and perhaps did not appropriately report the significance of his rival balloonists' impact (Scott 7).

The first U.S. balloon program since the Civil War was authorized in 1892 as the Balloon Section of the U.S. Signal Corps (van Eaton 6).

New Experiments

The Great Exhibition in 1851 in London was intended as a glorification of British power, and it established the international exhibition as an important phenomenon, a way to display technology, industry and national pride before the establishment of the World's Fair. One feature was a gallery of balloons, and attendance during the event was very large.

The French artist who called himself Nadar seems to have done some photography from a balloon, although no photos have survived. Nadar was an important pioneer in various aspects of photography, and also like P.T. Barnum in that he was adept at generating publicity about himself and his projects. One such project, in 1863, was constructing a large balloon. Nadar had it designed by Louis and Jules Godard (two more members of a family that produced many balloonists). Called the *Geant,* the craft took 212,000 cubic feet of gas to fill and was 196 feet high. The wicker gondola was as large as a small cottage, and a flight launched from Paris on October 4 carried 15 people. It came down near Meaux after a flight of five hours, though the flight was supposed to have lasted longer.

Nadar tried again on October 18 with only six passengers, and the flight got as far as Hanover in Germany before descending. The end of the flight reads like satire on ballooning, as wind blew the deflated balloon along the ground, ripping the limbs off trees, plowing the ground, tearing apart telegraph lines, and being dragged across railroad tracks only seconds ahead of an express train. The balloon was finally stopped by tangling in a grove of trees. Passengers were banged up, and the huge balloon was destroyed, but miraculously no one was killed (Holmes 117-119).

The most remarkable use of balloons in the second half of the 19th century came during the Franco-Prussian War of 1870-1871. This war is sometimes forgotten, but its political consequences were immense. It toppled the French Emperor Napoleon III, whose regime was eventually replaced by a Republic. The Prussians led the German armed forces, which included the military of Prussia and a number of other German kingdoms and principalities, and in 1871, the German Empire was proclaimed, with the Prussian king becoming the German Kaiser.

The first use of balloons was not in Paris, but the large fortress city of Metz, where the Prussians had trapped and surrounded Marshal Bazaine's French Army before inflicting a stunning defeat on a France that was commonly thought to have had the world's best army. An officer conceived the idea of sending messages over the Prussian lines by using a small balloon, and the idea was approved by the trapped army's Pharmacist in Chief, perhaps because he knew about chemicals and gas. Small balloons were constructed of tracing paper coated with varnish. 14 balloons were sent carrying several thousand letters, and about half got through (Allaz 14).

The success with these small balloons led to the construction of larger balloons. They used town gas and could carry 30,000 letters. Sending messages was opened up to civilians as well as military personnel, and somewhere between 7-10 of the balloons were launched. Several of them fell into the Prussian lines, giving the besiegers very valuable information about morale in the city. Metz surrendered on October 27 (Allaz 14-15).

The Prussian army surrounded and besieged Paris in the Fall of 1870. The huge capital city was cut off from the outside, but the success of balloons at Metz inspired the Parisians. French ingenuity soon came up with ways to create balloons. During the course of the siege, 66 balloons were launched from Paris, and quite amazingly, 58 of them made it safely past the Prussian lines into the French countryside.

These balloons were manufactured to a standard surprisingly rigorous for a surrounded city. French engineers were then probably the world's best, and the balloon dimensions were set at

15.75 meters in diameter, with a capacity of 3,045 cubic meters of gas. They were to have a payload of 500 kilograms, made of good quality cloth varnished with linseed oil, and provided with a net made of tarred rope. The gondola was tiny, 1.4 by 1.1 by 1.1 meters (Allaz 16).

Remarkably, the regular postal service was merged into the balloon system, and the mail was standardized. Citizens were charged 20 centimes for letters going to France or Algeria, and the letters had to weigh under 4 grams. Postcards were standardized and cost the sender 10 centimes. Even more remarkably, most of this mail got through—over—the siege, and most of it got delivered to the recipient. Receiving a letter from a friend or relative in a besieged city may be a unique historical experience. In effect, this was the world's first air mail (Allaz 16).

From September 23, 1870-January 28, 1871, the balloons carried 10,700 kilograms of mail, 400 carrier pigeons, and 102 passengers, not counting the 66 aeronauts. Remarkably, more than 90% of the mail got through and was delivered. The carrier pigeons were supposed to carry messages back into Paris, but only 55 made it back. One intriguing aspect of using these carrier pigeons was that the French devised an early version of microfiche so that one bird could carry a large number of messages back to Paris. The spectacular success rate of the balloons was related to the fact that France had by far the largest and most experienced group of balloonists in the world, many of whom were in Paris at the start of the siege (Allaz 16).

The most spectacular single balloon exploit came on October 7. Minister of the Interior Léon Gambetta was a balloon passenger, escaped the city and the Prussians, and, after landing, began to form a resistance government. Gambetta's daring escape enhanced his reputation, and later he became a very important figure in French politics (Murphy 12).

Gambetta

The siege ended with an armistice, and while France avoided total chaos, Paris soon descended into perhaps its worst period before World War II with the rise of the Paris Commune. Whatever unity that had existed in the face of the Prussians vanished, and a quite gory revolution and repression followed.

Happier days came in a few years. The Paris *Exposition Universelle* of 1878 was designed to show the world the glories of France and French products. The Exposition featured a huge tethered balloon, 220 feet high and with 900,000 cubic feet of gas capacity. This craft is said to have a lift of 27 tons and could lift 50 people at a time. Appropriately named the *Mammoth*, during the Exposition it lofted more than 35,000 sightseers several hundred feet up (Holmes 210). While there are no figures, these 35,000 passengers may well have been equivalent in total to all the aeronauts and all the passengers that came before. It suggested that air transportation might be part of the future.

Pictures of the balloon

In 1874, the French Republic formally added a Balloon Corps to its military. This may seem to be just a detail, but it means there was official recognition of the potential of balloons, and the other major powers quickly followed the French example (Murphy 12).

Balloons were of some interest to the nascent science of meteorology, particularly in exploring the atmosphere. One important scientific balloon flight resulted in tragedy in 1875, when three French scientists rose to an altitude of nearly 28,000 feet. Only one of the three survived, as the other two died of aviation hypoxia. This made it clear that the equipment of the day could not keep aeronauts alive five miles up.

The U.S. used a balloon during the Spanish-American War. In Cuba, a U.S. Signal Corps balloon was able to confirm that the Spanish fleet was in Santiago harbor, important information because the public was spooked by the fact that the location of the Spanish fleet had previously been unknown. However, this balloon, named the *Santiago,* actually became a hazard in combat. During the attack on the Cuban city, American troops became bunched up and the balloon was tethered near the troops. Spanish artillery fired at the area indicated by the balloon's tether, causing casualties. The *Santiago* itself was brought down by Spanish rifle fire (Ullman 125). The U.S. does not seem to have used balloons in the occupation of Puerto Rico, or the conflict in the Philippines.

Balloons were used for military purposes by the British in the Boer War in South Africa, by Japan and Russia in the Russo-Japanese War of 1903-1905, and by the French in various colonial campaigns in Africa, but the basic problem with balloons since their creation was that a flexible envelope made any balloon susceptible to wind, and in high wind, observations might be impossible. An observer in a gyrating gondola would be too busy holding on for dear life to make useful notes on enemy positions.

The problem was partly solved in 1898 when German engineers devised a sausage-shaped balloon equipped with fins or vanes at one end. This resulted in greater balloon stability in wind and bad weather, and it obviously improved the quality of any observations made. Called the *Drachen*, the German design was quickly adopted by the other powers (Murphy 13).

A *Drachen*

Balloons were a technology easily adaptable to fiction. As early as the 1780s, *The Adventures of Baron Munchausen* featured a tall tale about the baron using a balloon at night to mischievously relocate a castle while the inhabitants were asleep. Perhaps the first novel prominently featuring balloons was a pioneering and inventive work of science fiction, written by 20-year-old Jane Loudon in 1827. *The Mummy: A Tale of the Twenty First Century* had a balloon that folded into a size that fits into a desk drawer, but when unfolded, it would conveniently transport three passengers to Egypt. Jules Verne wrote *Five Weeks in a Balloon* in 1863 about a fictional flight from Zanzibar to Senegal. Mark Twain's 1894 *Tom Sawyer Abroad* had Tom, Huckleberry Finn, and Jim flying across Africa to Mt. Sinai, a sort of satire of Verne's novel.

Other than exploiting their military and scientific potential, ballooning remained largely entertainment, so it attracted adventurers and what might be described as hobbyists. The career of Mexico's first native balloonist illustrates this.

Benito Leon Acosta made his first ascent in April 1842, and his balloons generated a great deal of public interest. One of his benefactors was Santa Anna, Mexico's on-and-off dictator for two decades. Santa Anna awarded Acosta a three-year monopoly on balloon launches anywhere in Mexico. As with many dictators, Santa Anna liked to present public spectacles, with himself as benefactor to the people. His program of grandiosity seems to have worked because, despite repeated disasters and losing wars, Santa Anna kept returning to power. After some serious accidents, Acosta retired in 1855. He lived to a ripe old age, and he would sometimes make small hot air balloons to entertain children (Kuhn 115-16).

Mexico's most famous balloonist was Joaquin de la Cantolla y Rico. Aside from hundreds of ascents, he tested a dirigible prototype, but it didn't work. In his age, he became a bit of an eccentric, walking about town in a top hat, telling stories about his quite real adventures, and fascinating children with his glass eye, the consequence of a crash landing (Kuhn 117-18).

Other forms of entertainment merged with balloons, and the public interest remained intense enough for aeronautical spectacles to be mildly profitable. The continued underlying feature was the presence of danger. For example, one famous Mexican daredevil entertainer was Tranquileno Aleman, who performed on a trapeze suspended from a balloon. He did hundreds of performances, but his luck ran out in 1889 in Cuernavaca when he fell from the trapeze (Kuhn 117).

The Development of Airships

As noted earlier, the Jesuit Lana de Terzi proposed an airship in 1670. His concept was suspending a real fighting ship from four copper spheres from which the air had been removed (Murphy 3). He and Leonardo seem to have been the first to have thought in terms of an actual ship in the air. Terzi's airship had masts and sails, anchors and cannons, a bowsprit and keel. The term "airship" is significant because of the historical baggage of the word "ship." An airship took nautical terminology into the air, sailing in the atmosphere in a real version of Roger Bacon's long-ago vision.

Airships are defined as lighter than aircraft with a semi-rigid or rigid structure and some means of self-propulsion. The crucial difference between airships and balloons is the ability of an airship to be steered and to overcome the balloon's vulnerability to wind and weather. In a way, it's the difference between a raft and a boat with oars. Balloons can be small or large, but steering and navigation possibilities have always been limited. Airships can be small or enormous, and power and steering allowed vastly more potential.

A major engineering problem in developing airships was devising an engine that could power the ship but that was light enough not to offset a lot of the craft's lifting capacity. The first such airship carrying an engine was devised by a French engineer named Henri Giffard, who became interested in powered flight, and how to overcome the air resistance that made balloons difficult to control and very difficult to navigate along any sort of regular flight path. As an engineer, he was able to envision solutions that took the form of a non-rigid but shaped airship 140 feet long with a maximum diameter of 40 feet, and pointed at each end so the envelope's construction gave it a navigable shape. The balloon held 88,000 cubic feet of hydrogen, and a gondola was suspended under it.

Giffard

Giffard built a three-horsepower steam engine, based on a boiler that burned coke, with precautions against sparks, which were a serious danger with the highly combustible hydrogen. The engine powered a three-bladed propeller. The airship reached 3,000 feet and achieved a speed of about six miles per hour. It worked, but it only worked in calm conditions with no winds (Murphy 14).

This aptly named "aerial steamer" flew for about 15 miles on September 24, 1852 (van Eaton 4). Giffard's experiment was in its way to becoming highly successful, but nothing came of the pioneering flight. That the airship could only be used during conditions of absolute calm may have been one reason. Another factor probably was the realization that Giffard's type of engine was highly dangerous in conjunction with hydrogen gas.

A model of Giffard's dirigible

   During the Franco-Prussian War, the French naval engineer Henri Dupuy de Lôme devised a highly unusual airship design. The war ended before any prototype was constructed, but in 1872 he built a craft 49 feet long, with a 46 foot maximum diameter, a 123,000 cubic foot capacity and a four-bladed propeller 29 feet long. The most unusual feature of this design was that the propeller was powered by a crew of eight using a hand crank. One historian dryly observed that the crew was powered by rum (Murphy 14). The airship did manage short flights, which is surprising, and the method of power was much like the hand-crank-powered Confederate submarine CSS *Hunley*.

A depiction of the airship

The next powered flight of an airship a semi-rigid craft over Vienna in 1872, using an internal combustion engine designed by Paul Haenlein. The engine was powered by coal gas (Smith 147).

In October 1883, Albert and Gaston Tissandier flew another French airship design, this time powered by a 1.5 horsepower electric engine (Smith 147). Electric engines were potentially much less dangerous in common with hydrogen than other kinds of engines.

The year 1884 brought another French airship design. Army Captains Charles Renard and Arthur Krebs, both engineers, built *La France*. At 165 feet long, this rather large airship was driven by an 8.5 horsepower electric engine based on a battery system. The ship was essentially an early dirigible and the design was promising, but lack of funding killed the effort (Murphy 15). Batteries in this period were heavy and expensive, but the technology was quickly improving.

One technological development in 1885 profoundly affected airship development. Germany's Gottlieb Daimler designed an effective internal combustion engine. Yet another technology was a new process for producing aluminum, which soon allowed a lightweight means of giving airships some framework structure.

As internal combustion engines were improved, the power versus weight ratio became more and more favorable for airships (and also for heavier than air machines, then in an early but intense stage of development). The first use of an internal combustion engine in an airship came in 1885, when Friedrich Wölfert used one to power an airship of his own design. Wölfert was a German clergyman, illustrating that non-professional enthusiasts still had important contributions to make. Professional engineers and designers did not yet dominate aviation.

Perhaps the most colorful of the pioneer airship designers was the Brazilian Alberto Santos-Dumont. He came from a family wealthy enough to support his interest in airships and aircraft, and after moving to Paris, he designed and built several small airships in 1898. He moored one of his airships, Number Nine, outside his Paris apartment and also outside his favorite restaurant (Murphy 16).

In one of his early flights, with dirigible Number 1, he rose to 1,300 feet before the airship lost gas and drifted down. Santos-Dumont yelled at some boys playing in a field to grab the guide rope and run into the wind. They did, and he landed safely. He collected all the parts, put them in the wicker basket gondola and then caught a cab back to Paris (Hiam 18).

It made for a great story, but it's easy to wonder how all the ropes, the envelope, the rudder, propeller and the other gear fit into a basket or a taxi cab. The cheerful story seems somewhat improbable, and perhaps many of the stories about him are. His colorful personal life cloaked an aeronautical genius with a taste for danger. He also was a master writer, and reading his tales provides a zesty sense of adventure a century later.

To be fair, Santos-Dumont continued his eccentric experiments with increasing seriousness and increasing significance in the next several years. His Number 6 was used in his most famous exploit. There was a cash prize called the Deutsch Prize of 100,000 Francs for an airship to fly from the suburb of St. Cloud to and around the Eiffel Tower and back in under a half hour.

On October 19, 1901, Santos-Dumont took off for Paris in an attempt to win this prize. He made it, circled the Eiffel Tower, and started back, but his engine sputtered and stopped nd then started again. He made it back to the starting point with some 30 seconds to spare. His reputation was enhanced when he gave part of the prize to the poor in Paris and the rest to the employees who had built his airships (Hiam 19-20).

Around the same time, Ferdinand Graf von Zeppelin was experimenting with airships. Zeppelin had been a military observer for the Duchy of Wurttenburg, one of a number of independent German states, during the American Civil War. He had ascended with Union observation balloons and was apparently impressed with their utility, and he was the only person among these airship pioneers who actually had experience in the use of balloons under battlefield conditions.

Ballooning continued to attract attention, and as the 19th century ended, something of an extreme era of ballooning commenced. It was characterized by the search for records to break, deliberately risky exploits to entertain onlookers, and sheer recklessness (Holmes 212-213). A typical exploit was a flight by the Count de la Vaux. Lifting off during yet another Paris exposition, this flight lasted 35 hours and the balloon landed near Kiev in Russia. The flight covered 1,195 miles, breaking a distance record set in 1859 (Fischer 5).

As the great era of ballooning was coming to its end, airship developers were busy. In 1900, an experimental Zeppelin flew over Lake Constance. Significantly, the craft had an aluminum frame and was powered by a Daimler engine (Holmes 210).

Zeppelin

One of the first Zeppelins

By 1899, it was clear that airborne attacks were going to become practical military options in the near future. In fact, the American delegate to the 1899 Hague Convention pushed for a ban on balloons dropping bombs, on the grounds that bombs dropped from a drifting balloon were impossible to aim accurately and might accidentally hit civilians. The ban was adopted, but in a somewhat surprising twist, the ban was only for five years, because it was assumed that within five years, airships like the Zeppelins being developed would be so accurate in dropping bombs that the ban would no longer be needed (Ziegler 751-752).

Needless to say, the next generation of aerial technology and wars would prove that thinking remarkably shortsighted.

Airships and Balloons in World War I

Zeppelin retired in 1890 with a relatively undistinguished military career despite achieving the rank of general, so his motivation for developing his airships seems to have been simple patriotism. He started experimenting with airships, seeing in them military utility for future conflicts. He had no way of knowing that the airships he created would come to be known by his family name, or that the word Zeppelin would be applied to new designs of airships well over a century after his death.

LZ-1, Count von Zeppelin's experimental airship that flew over Lake Constance, embodied previous concepts of airships and recent experience with real airships dating back 50 years. LZ-1 was built in a floating hangar on Lake Constance, but it was poorly designed and lacked stability. It was huge at 420 feet long and 38 feet in diameter, with an outer envelope of an aluminum-zinc alloy. It had a capacity of 400,000 cubic feet, and only three test flights were necessary to demonstrate that the structure was simply not strong enough.

It would be another five years before the LZ-2 and LZ-3 appeared. Zeppelin received support from a public lottery, but he had to mortgage his wife's property. LZ-2 was promising, but it was destroyed by a storm while on the ground. LZ-3 added fins for stability, and the internal structure was enhanced. LZ-4 in 1908 made a 12-hour flight over Switzerland and caused a sensation. In July 1908, the king and queen of Wurttemberg were passengers on the fifth flight of LZ-4.

LZ-4

The government offered financial support if one of Zeppelin's ships could make a flight lasting 24 hours, and Zeppelin accepted the challenge, but on the flight, the airship went to ground and burned. This might have ended Zeppelin's projects, but the idea of airships appealed to the German public and they quickly donated 6 million marks, a remarkable sum that allowed Zeppelin to continue developing an airship that performed to expectations.

The airships had more than military utility. Even as Zeppelin continued his work, the world's first airline was founded in 1909. DELAG (Deutsch Luftschiffahrts Aktiengessellschaft) operated flights from Berlin to Friedrichshafen, with the run taking 4-9 hours, compared to 18-24 hours by train. Nearly 10,000 passengers were carried without an injury until the line was closed upon the outbreak of World War I. DELAG resumed operations at the end of the war, but its two airships were confiscated by the Allies as war reparations.

While balloons had long had a connection with advertising and serving as flying billboards, one of the more interesting came in 1909 when a balloon in Britain bore, "Votes for Women." Suffragist Muriel Matters hired the balloon with the intent of dropping suffragist pamphlets on a procession to Westminster that included King Edward VIII, and Matters was in the basket with an aeronaut and was intending to toss her pamphlets on the royal procession. The balloon went astray and ended tangled in a tree, but the feminist flight did achieve plenty of publicity.

Matters

THE SUCCESSFUL START FOR WESTMINSTER,
Which Ended in Failure to Reach Their Destination.

A picture of the flight

In the decade leading up to World War I, the nations of Europe were looking to the skies and considering how real, functional military airpower would look. For Germany, the process of turning these considerations into a reality began when the Military Board bought the first in a series of Zeppelin dirigible airships in 1907. In 1910, the first planes were added to the army, and a Naval Air Service (NAS) was founded the following year. In 1912, the army's air arm was turned into the Military Aviation Service (MAS), though this remained separate from the NAS. The French army obtained a dirigible in 1905, and after the Germans had previously solved some of the aerodynamic problems affecting tethered observation balloons by altering the shape from spherical to sausage-like and adding fins at the rear, that design, which the Germans called the *drachen*, was quickly adopted by other militaries.

Around the same time, the Italians made the first practical use of airpower during their 1911-12 invasion of Libya. During this campaign, a small number of aircraft were used to reconnoiter the enemy, direct artillery, and drop bombs. Still, the Italians lacked the resources to build a substantial air force, and as a result, Germany was fast becoming the global leader. By 1914, the NAS had 36 aircraft and the MAS had 250. In only five years, military planes had gone from non-existent to a significant and sizable fighting force, one whose potential had been demonstrated in the field by the Italians. Most of Germany's competitors had only around 50 aircraft, compared with their 300.

On the other side of the Atlantic, the U.S. Army Signal Corps got a balloon in 1905 at Fort Meyer in Virginia, and in 1908, it bought an airship designed by Thomas Baldwin. The Navy got its first aircraft in 1911 and its first airship in 1915. These were hydrogen airships, and the U.S.

did not switch from hydrogen to the safer helium until 1921. The Americans did not join the Allied Powers in the war until 1917, and by then most American equipment was outdated.

In 1909, there was a balloon panic in Britain and widespread understanding that things were changing. The Germans were developing a modern naval fleet that seemed likely to significantly challenge the Royal Navy, and the rapid development of the Zeppelins seemed to have people rattled. H.G. Wells' novel *The War in the Air* appeared as a serial in the January 1908 edition of *Pall Mall Gazette*, becoming the most famous literary work ever written that involves airships (although the airpower described included both airships and aircraft). The novel was actually about a surprise German air attack on the United States, rather than Britain, but a British character named Bert Smallways winds up in Germany on the eve of the attack and is somehow taken along, He sees the wipeout of a battleship fleet and the bombing of New York. A Confederation of East Asia (China and Japan) launches a surprise attack from the Pacific and lands a million men. Complications include air fighting in Europe, and the Asian forces invading the Middle East. The world economic system collapses as war breaks the world's political system.

The plot is both contrived and overly complicated, yet it clearly channeled some things people were concerned about at the start of the 20th century. Japan had just defeated Russia in the Russo-Japanese War, and air attacks seemed to render the English Channel useless as defense, so it was clear that the novel touched a nerve.

In the wake of Wells' story, the media discussed at length the danger of an aerial invasion by the Germans. One journalist speculated that the Germans could transport 350,000 men from Calais to Dover in a single night.

The peak of the scare came in March and April 1909, when people in various parts of Britain reported seeing mysterious airships. There was widespread paranoia that the Germans were up to something, and that it had to do with airships and invading Britain. There was speculation that Germans working in Britain were really soldiers in disguise (Golin 45-49).

While those fears were unfounded, the progress of Zeppelin development was indeed rapid, and it concerned the British, so they decided to buy a Zeppelin if possible. In 1912, they sent two officers, including Colonel Mervyn O'Gorman, disguised as Americans to review airships in French, German, Austrian and Italian facilities (Higham 68).

O'Gorman

Even as planes were being manufactured at increasing rates, training for pilots remained primitive ahead of World War I. Without the experience of extensive aerial combat, there was little understanding of the maneuvers a plane could make or the problems it would face when pushed to its limits. There was no body of tactical or flying knowledge to draw upon, and no philosophy of aerial warfare. Furthermore, the pilots themselves were drawn from the officer corps, meaning they were mostly bored young men looking for a bit of excitement. The high risk of accidents in these new flying machines contributed to a culture of boisterous thrill-seeking that gave them a poor reputation with the rest of the military.

Furthermore, in 1914, airplanes, despite undergoing rapid developments, had a load limit of about 500 pounds, but the 1914 edition of Zeppelins could carry 20,000 pounds. This meant the Zeppelin could carry a crew of 16, 1,100 pounds of bombs and enough fuel for about thirty hours of continuing operations. Despite the obvious difference, the German Kaiser and the Chief of the Naval Staff at first envisioned the Zeppelin not as an offensive weapon, but in a defensive reconnaissance role (Robinson 130-132).

Aside from minor exceptions and a major exception of the Battle of Jutland, the Royal Navy kept the expensive German Navy bottled up in its bases for nearly the entire war, and with the

High Seas Fleet rusting away in port, the envisioned Zeppelin role as scout and reconnaissance for naval operations diminished.

The only effective available means of striking back at Britain proper was by air, and Zeppelins offered an obvious way to make that strike. The belligerent powers had already been acquiring aircraft for potential uses, but given that aerial warfare had never been a major component of any conflict, it's understandable that few on either side had any idea what the planes were capable of doing. Furthermore, at the start of the war, all sides' aircraft were ill-equipped for combat mostly because the idea that planes might somehow fight was still a novel one, and the adaptations had not yet been developed that would allow the aerial battles later in the war. As a result, aircraft were used almost entirely for reconnaissance early on, allowing generals to gain unprecedented levels of information about enemy movements.

Adding to the already hideous risks of flying their tiny, fragile aircraft, the pilots of 1914 had no recognition symbols on their aircraft, nor had soldiers received training in aircraft recognition – a difficult task considering that each side fielded dozens of different types of airplanes simultaneously, and that a given design typically became obsolete and underwent replacement by a radically different airframe every 5-6 months. Until recognition symbols came into use about year into the war, soldiers on all sides opened fire whenever they spotted an airplane overhead, automatically assuming it to be an enemy craft. This reflex proved so ingrained that on one occasion German troops shot down one of their own bombing Zeppelins shortly after its takeoff, even though the British did not use Zeppelins of that type and only employed tethered or "captive" balloons.

As that anecdote suggests, the Germans eventually came around to the idea of using Zeppelins to bomb enemy targets. Bombs were dropped on Paris in August 1914, and Zeppelins bombed Belgian forces as the Germans advanced on Liège. On the other side, British pilots destroyed a Zeppelin on the ground at Düsseldorf. This was bombing at its most simple, as the explosives kept on hooks on the side of the machines and dropped by a crew member by hand. These small forays into aerial bombardment barely hinted at the bombing campaigns to come.

Picture of a Zeppelin during the war

Picture of a crater left by a Zeppelin bomb in Paris during the war

The first Zeppelin raid on Britain came on January 19, 1915, with three airships launching, but only two making it to the target. L-3 dropped six 110-pound bombs and some incendiaries, and L-4 scattered its munitions over rural Norfolk. Both airships iced up on the way home, but 4 Britons were killed and 16 injured, and the German public relished the news of the attack. The first attack on London proper came on May 31, 1915, when LZ-38 flew in at 10,000 feet and dropped 3,000 pounds of bombs, killing 7 and injuring 35 (Robinson 136, 138). LZ-38 would be destroyed by British bombs targeting its hangar less than half a year later.

While the German public enjoyed the fact that the war was being carried to the British, in Britain the attacks were seen as evidence of German brutality. It also shocked the British public and created further demand that the homeland be better protected. Therein lay the main military impact of the Zeppelin attacks: the damage inflicted was insignificant, but the demand for homeland defense did divert weapons, aircraft, and personnel from the actual battle front in France. Reports of Zeppelin raids on Britain encouraged German national morale, but that was counteracted by British unity when faced with attacks.

Indeed, there are some parallels between attacks by Zeppelins and the U-boat campaigns. Both were dependent on stealth, both were almost entirely Navy ventures, and because of the difficulty identifying targets, both necessarily were indiscriminate in the casualties they caused.

The Germans also set up an innovative radio navigation system. The airships called up the stations, which took bearings and radioed the airships back, but the British discovered they could listen in and use some of the information to anticipate the Zeppelins and make sure they had a warm reception. The relatively slow speed of the airships meant that the defense had time to organize itself.

The Zeppelins were obviously huge targets, so they did not attack during the full moon because they were too easily seen. Darkness gave the airships a considerable measure of protection, as it was difficult to see them, and it took some time before interception aircraft developed the skills of flying at night. In short order, however, defenses against the airships improved and powerful searchlights proved their worth. Furthermore, due to their vast quantities of hydrogen, Zeppelins were quite vulnerable. When LZ-37 was caught in daylight near Ghent in Belgium, it was bombed from overhead and caught fire. It fell, but its lucky crew escaped. Many crews did not survive.

A contemporary artist's depiction of LZ-37's destruction

Most attacks by the German airships caused little damage and few casualties, but the most damaging attack on London came on September 8, 1915. This attack, consisting of three Zeppelins, was commanded by Heinrich Mathy, who later said he aimed for the Bank of England. Incendiaries dropped during this raid started major fires in warehouses and in an industrial area. In October, another raid resulted in 38 people killed and 87 injured, the largest casualty toll of any of the raids (Robinson 139). These raids were dwarfed by bombing raids in World War II, especially during the Blitz against the British, but there was still a sense of outrage over civilian casualties during the early stages of World War I.

Mathy

Several Zeppelin raids involved a bigger number of airships. In January 1916, seven airships attacked Manchester and Liverpool, and the British countered by increasing antiaircraft defenses and instituting blackouts. Later in 1916, new model Zeppelins attacked with up to 9,000 pounds of bombs, and that September, one raid consisted of an attack using 12 Navy and 4 Army airships, the only attack during the war with airships from both services participating. Problems in coordinating and airship losses resulted in the German Army deciding to no longer use airships for attacking Britain; from then on, the Army would rely on new Gotha bombers. Thus, almost all attacks on Britain came from Navy airships.

The British developed an incendiary bullet designed to counter Zeppelins by igniting the hydrogen. On September 3, 1916, Zeppelin SL-11 was attacked at 12,000 feet by a BE,2c fighter piloted by William Robinson. A crowd that some observers thought might have numbered a million watched the Zeppelin's destruction in the sky, and Britons rejoiced over the demise of an airship some called a "baby killer."

THE END OF THE "BABY-KILLER".

A British postcard celebrating SL-11's demise

The last raid of 1916, on November 27, involved 10 airships, and two of them, L-34 and L-21, were shot down by fighter interceptors. The shoot-downs could be spectacular as the hydrogen ignited, but it was a hideous death for those who served as crewmembers.

A major incident occurred in Germany itself in late 1917 at the Althorn base. In a series of explosions, five airships and the four hangars that housed them were destroyed. The cause of the disaster was never discovered, but there was no evidence of sabotage.

The last Zeppelin raid took place on August 5, 1918, during which the commander of the Zeppelin program was killed when his airship was shot down. As odd as it may sound, the commander was known to be despondent, and there is speculation that this could have been suicide by Zeppelin (Robinson 143-145).

Naturally, Zeppelin technology developed as the war continued. The L-49 was commissioned in 1917 and could reach 20,000 feet, well above the altitude limit for defensive fighter aircraft interceptors. The ship was 644 feet long, 78 feet in diameter, and had a capacity of almost 2 million cubic feet of hydrogen. This ship had a useful lift of 87,000 pounds and was powered by five 240-horsepower Maybach engines. The L-49 could carry three tons of bombs.

This advanced Zeppelin made one bombing run on Britain in October 1917, only to be blown off course and come to ground in France, where it was captured intact. L-49 became a kind of prototype for the later USS *Shenandoah* (Murphy 131). One can only conclude that the materials and labor going into this ill-fated airship would have been far better devoted to producing more fighter or bomber aircraft.

L-49

The redesign traded altitude for other factors. One less engine was used, weakening the airships' ability to maneuver in wind and lessening the bomb carrying capacity. Crews experienced discomfort at 20,000 feet, which made the already imprecise business of dropping bombs even more difficult, to the point where hitting any target worth the effort was essentially a coincidence.

All in all, during the war the Zeppelins dropped a total of about 5,800 bombs, killing 557 people and injuring 1,358. Of the 50 or so Navy Zeppelin crews trained, about 40% were killed in combat on other operations, meaning that about as many Zeppelin crewmembers died as the victims of their raids. About 35 airships were used by the German Army, mostly on the Eastern Front and in the Balkans (Robinson 147).

One Zeppelin flight has become legendary. The LZ-59 was designated to carry supplies to the German forces in East Africa. Known as the Schutztruppe, the German forces were led by the also legendary commander von Lettow-Vorbeck, whose mostly African soldiers fought a campaign that covered much of East Africa (what is now Tanzania was then a German colony). The airship flew to a German base in Bulgaria, was loaded for a long trip, and, in November 1917, embarked on what is still probably the longest mission ever undertaken by an airship in a time of war. Loaded with everything from a medical team and machine guns to Iron Crosses, the LZ-59 crossed the Mediterranean and flew over Egypt (then a British colony and military base) on to a point in the middle of Sudan. The airship turned back because British intelligence got the German Navy to believe that the Schutztruppe had lost the only available ground it controlled where a Zeppelin could land. The original plan had been for the Zeppelin to land and then be recycled in some militarily useful way, as there would have been no replenishment hydrogen available for the return trip.

The LZ-59 later was sent to attack the British base at Malta, but the ship was lost with all hands, apparently as part of an accident.

LZ-59

While the principal employment of Zeppelins in the war consisted reconnaissance and bombing raids by Navy airships against Britain, the German Army used a number of Zeppelins, a few of which were stationed in Bulgaria (a German ally), to raid Salonica in Greece, where an Allied expeditionary force was bottled up by Bulgarian and German forces. They also bombed

Bucharest when Romania entered the war on the Allied side. Army Zeppelins early in the war bombed Paris and Antwerp, and there were plans to bomb Petrograd (as St. Petersburg, Russia's capital, had been renamed so it was a less German form of a name). The plan was frustrated by bad weather and accidents before it was finally called off.

While Zeppelins were more intriguing airships, the less complicated observation balloons were far more militarily significant and far more numerous. Observation balloons were tethered and lifted by hydrogen, functioning at altitudes from a few hundred feet to 7,000 feet or more. They generally were stationed at some distance behind the lines and protected by anti-aircraft guns once the sides realized airplanes could shoot them down.

The balloons were important for two particular reasons. The first was to keep an eye on the enemy by simply observing enemy activity and to map out positions. The second was to assist the artillery by reporting the accuracy of fire and spotting targets. In this war, artillery was the big killer, and most artillery fire was shot over the horizon at unseen targets. Thus, artillery observers were crucial (Strekfuss 54-57).

Getting messages from the observers in the balloons to the ground in a timely manner was important. All kinds of communication were tried, including signal flags, flares, and notes tossed to the ground in weighted containers. As the war went on, telephone connections between balloon and ground became common, and there was considerable development of radio communications. Usually associated with later wars, electronic warfare had its beginnings here. The Germans tried jamming Allied radio communications, and the Allies developed countermeasures (Strekfuss 80).

Balloons had an advantage over observation aircraft because the balloons stayed aloft far longer. This advantage declined as the technical capacity of airplanes increased and the importance of aerial photography became more and more important, but it also ensured balloons would constantly be targeted by enemy forces.

In fact, thanks to the relatively static front lines, World War I's balloons represented an even greater asset than those of the American Civil War, which featured far more fluid, mobile warfare. Whole lines of balloons watched over specific sectors of the front, watching for troop concentrations indicating an approaching offensive. With these floating observation platforms constantly on the watch, communicating with the ground via early field telephones, commanders frequently targeted the balloon lines during the later war. A row of 15 balloons spaced miles apart could cover an immense area of front. Thus, destroying them enabled a general to mass an attack unobserved – or could serve as a feint, leading the enemy to think an offensive approached the area of balloon destruction when in fact the blow would fall far away.

During the early part of the war, the British and French continued to use round balloons, while the Germans deployed a design known as the *Drachen*, a long, cylindrical, sausage-shaped structure with greater stability than the spherical balloon. The Germans added a single stabilizing fin underneath the *Drachen*, an appendage irreverently dubbed the "testicle" by German troops.

The French soon adopted the elongated cylindrical shape and improved on it, fitting each of their airships with three stabilizing fins at the rear – one underneath and one on either side. This design, the *Caquot,* named after its inventor, Captain Albert Caquot, proved even more stable even in most gale-strength winds. The Germans, in turn, copied the improved design, though they continued to call it a *Drachen,* rather confusingly.

A Caquot balloon during the war

Filled with hydrogen, these balloons made prime targets for enemy aircraft. Accordingly, each "balloon nest" featured impressive defenses. The crew tethered their balloon to a massive, powered winch on the ground. In the event of an attack, a ground crew turned on the winch motor, yanking the balloon swiftly out of the sky. Adding extra precautions, a full ring of anti-aircraft artillery surrounded each balloon nest.

As the balloon descended, any attacking airplanes found themselves forced to either give up or fly into short range of the bristling ring of AAA already firing on them. Fighters would also scramble to intercept and kill the intruders before they returned to their own lines, regardless of the success or failure of the anti-balloon attack. With more space in the balloon for secondary equipment, most balloonists had parachutes, which could not fit into aircraft of the era. A balloonist stood a good chance of bailing out and surviving any attack that left him alive and uninjured.

Despite the nearly suicidal danger involved in attacking a balloon, some men developed "balloon fever," an intense hunting urge directed at the balloons. The French assembled whole squadrons of these men, who often worked together in a team effort to bring down balloons, while other balloon hunting pilots preferred to work alone.

The French also created the first rocket-armed aircraft for the purpose of destroying balloons. The incendiary rockets very frequently set off a devastating conflagration in the hydrogen if they hit, but misses far outnumbered hits with the unguided rockets. Resembling big fireworks rockets with a long sticks or tails, the rockets launched from the interplane struts of a biplane's upper and lower wings with an electric current serving to set them off, the triggering cable being connected to a firing switch in the cockpit. Though they would touch off a balloon's hydrogen in a dramatic blast of fire if they struck home, most rockets missed, as French pilot Pierre de Cazenove de Pradines recounted in August 1917: "At the right moment, I pulled up, the rockets fired, and went in all directions in an impressive smoky display. When it cleared, I found myself flying at an intact balloon. The rockets had gone in every direction except at the target! I withdrew [...] The next day I returned with phosphorus bullets in my machine gun and flamed that balloon." (Guttman, 2005, 10).

While killing the observer in the basket remained relatively easy, the main objective of attacks on balloons lay in setting the blimp on fire, thereby destroying it for future use. This process, known as "sausage roasting," required precise technique and a large dash of luck. As de Pradines suggested in his writing, phosphorus bullets (tracers) provided the most reliable method of setting a balloon ablaze. However, even with this ammunition, the pilot needed to first rupture the balloon, then fire again into the area of the puncture, where escaping hydrogen blended with oxygen to produce a highly volatile mixture. Simply firing a burst into the blimp and then leaving seldom did more than produce a patchable leak.

While most men who developed "balloon fever" died quickly, shot down by the heavy fire defending the airships, a few survived to become "balloon aces," those who could claim five or more balloons destroyed. All of the medium and large combatants in the war deployed observation balloons, and all countries fielding significant numbers of aircraft produced at least a few balloon aces. The roll of known balloon aces adds up to just 73 men. Those who destroyed 10 or more balloons included one Belgian, 6 Frenchmen, 7 Germans, one South African, one American (Frank Luke), one Englishman (Henry Woollett), and one Irishman. The French and Germans had more balloon aces thanks to their powerful, effective aircraft designs.

At times, the opponents of specific aces went to extraordinary lengths to kill these individual men who proved adept at destroying their balloons. The British used a bizarre ruse to kill Rudolf von Eschwege, a tough-looking 22 year old potential balloon ace from Bad Homburg. Von Eschwege fought on the Macedonian Front, proving a chivalrous but deadly opponent who downed a confirmed total of 16 British aircraft, earning him the sobriquet of "the Eagle of the Aegean." A British pilot whom he had shot down, identified by history only as Lieutenant Hyde, later recalled the German's gallantry when he and the pilot of a two-seater shot down by Eschwege recuperated in German custody after being shot down: "Sydney Beare and I will always remember Eschwege's solicitude for us and our wounds. He brought us in hospital gifts of chocolate, books and cigarettes. May his soul rest in peace after his many flights." (Musciano, 1999, 54).

Von Eschwege

Von Eschwege caught "balloon fever" on October 28th, 1917 when he attacked a British blimp near Orljak close to the Struma River. Circling around to get the sun behind him, the Eagle of the Aegean roared in to the attack. Seeing the black shape of the Albatros D III boring in out of the glaring solar disc, the artillery observer in the basket slipped on his parachute and leaped over the side into the gulf of air to escape the coming hail of machine gun bullets.

As the parachute blossomed hundreds of feet below, von Eschwege opened fire with the incendiary bullets he had ordered loaded into the machine by the ground crew that morning, sending several bursts into the bloated sausage shape drifting on the early wind ahead of him. The balloon, however, did not catch fire. The German pilot returned again and again, until finally the balloon exploded into flames and crumpled towards the earth.

A group of Allied fighters attacked von Eschwege as he flew away, but the adroit German just managed to escape through a series of white-knuckled maneuvers. The experience, with its thrilling danger, technical challenges, and the spectacular sight of the huge blimp erupting into fire, seemed to capture the pilot's imagination.

For the brief remainder of his life, he appeared fixated on destroying balloons. Von Eschwege struck again on November 9th, killing the observer in a British balloon basket at Kopiva but finding himself unable to destroy the blimp due to jammed machine guns. Nevertheless, he returned to the site of his first victory, Orljak, on November 15th, attacking and destroying the replacement balloon launched by the British.

Just four days later, von Eschwege attacked a balloon at Kelendra. A 17th Squadron Sopwith 1 1/2 Strutter counterattacked the incoming Albatros, and von Eschwege dispatched the British pilot in a quick dogfight. However, this distraction gave the English time to winch their balloon all the way back to earth, putting it beyond the German pilot's reach. Accordingly, he attacked four other British fighters nearby, but they scattered, obliging him to return to base without any further kills.

On November 21st, von Eschwege returned again. The balloon appeared to be in place once more and he dived to the attack. As he swept past the balloon after setting it on fire, however, the basket suddenly detonated in a massive explosion, engulfing his aircraft in smoke and fire. The British, determined to kill him, had sent up a balloon manned only by a straw dummy and 500 lbs of remote-detonated explosive. The blast wrecked enough of the fragile Albatros that von Eschwege lost control and plummeted some 2,500 feet to the ground, ending in a crash that smashed both the airplane and pilot to pieces. The British apparently felt ashamed of this action; while several wrote accounts stating emphatically that it was a legitimate war ruse, they noted that the locally posted English pilots refused to celebrate his death. The English soon dropped a message on the German airfield: "To the Bulgarian-German Flying Corps in Drama. The officers of the Royal Flying Corps regret to announce that Ltn von Eschwege was killed while attacking the captive balloon. His personal belongings will be dropped over the lines some time during the next few days." (Musciano, 1999, 53). The British lived up to this promise and also included a photograph of British pilots carrying von Eschwege's coffin at the funeral with full military honors which they gave him. Had he survived, von Eschwege might have become a noted balloon ace on this front.

Ironically, the most prolific balloon ace of the war belonged to no major power but hailed from Belgium. Willy Coppens, a builder of land yachts and model aircraft, received combat pilot's training in England. Piloting an uncommon aircraft, a Hanriot HD 1, Coppens made a name as a daredevil by buzzing his parents' house in German-occupied Brussels, flying so low his father waved to him from a window.

A portrait of Coppens

Starting in May 1918, Coppens began attacking German *Drachen* balloons by preference, though in at least one case he could not ignite one because morning dew still drenched its surface. In that instance, his fire cut the tethering cable, causing the balloon to rocket upwards and strike his aircraft. The Hanriot tumbled over the edge of the balloon and hurtled towards the earth, stalled, but Coppens managed to restart the engine in time.

Coppens, who painted his entire aircraft blue, continued destroying *Drachen* with great frequency, and the Germans soon called him the "Blue Devil." The Germans attempted to use the same trick on him as the British had on von Eschwege, but the Belgian attacked their explosive-rigged balloon so rapidly and unexpectedly that it plunged to earth and then detonated among the crowd of men who had gathered to watch, strewing the ground with wounded and dying Germans.

The Belgian balloon ace, despite his avid nature on the hunt, directed no vindictive feelings towards his opponents, as one regretful statement from him reveals: "I just killed a brave man, and I killed him in the worst way I could. The balloon observer didn't jump – he kept firing at me with a little handgun. The burning balloon just swallowed him up." (Guttman, 2005, 86).

Coppens continued to run amok among the balloons, raising his score to an all-time record of 35 blimps destroyed. The Germans, desperate to put an end to his one-man extermination campaign against their *Drachen*, first doubled and then tripled the number of anti-aircraft weapons guarding each balloon in the sector where he operated.

Finally, on October 5, 1918, just slightly more than a month before the cessation of hostilities, the Germans' increased balloon defense firepower paid off. During his attack on the last balloon he set alight, a machine gun bullet smashed the bones in Coppens' left leg and severed the artery. With arterial blood pumping into the cockpit, Coppens somehow managed to fly back Allied lines, landing in a field near La Panne. The medics and surgeons managed to save Coppens' life, amputating his left leg to do so.

In the end, the balloon ace not only achieved the highest score of any of his select group of airmen, but he survived the war and lived until December 21st, 1986. Despite participating in one of World War I's deadliest forms of aerial combat, Coppens lived to the age of 96.

The top American balloon-buster was Frank Luke, who had a highly unusual and very short career. Overall, he shot down 18 German aircraft, including 14 balloons, in just 10 flights across two weeks. On his 10th flight, he shot down three balloons and was himself shot down. He survived the crash landing, but he was shot as he ran. This paroxysm of balloon killing on his last flight won him the Medal of Honor.

The sharp increase in all forms of war in the air can be seen in the increased of combatant inventories over the course of the war. Just the naval inventory makes the point, as the Royal Navy went from under 100 aircraft to over 3,000, and from 6 airships to 111. The German Navy started the war with 24 aircraft and 1 airship and ended with 1,500 aircraft, and 19 airships. The French Navy expanded from 8 aircraft to 1,264 and possessed 58 airships by war's end, while the U.S. Navy expanded from 54 aircraft and 2 balloons to 2,100 airplanes, 15 airships, and 200 balloons (Strekfuss 168).

In April 1917, Americans had enough rubberized cloth (for balloon envelopes) to make two balloons per week. By the Armistice in November of 1918, there was enough to produce 10 each day. U.S. Balloon Service statistics for the war documented 5,866 balloon ascents, and that American observers made 116 parachute jumps, 35 of them from balloons on fire (Strekfuss 68, 70).

The American Army had a total of 27 pursuit squadrons (fighters), 7 day/night bomber squadrons, 18 corps and Army observation squadrons, and 17 balloon companies. The U.S. Navy had 27 air stations around the French and British coasts, with a mix of aircraft and balloons, 17 of which were primarily focused on the U-boat menace (Strekfuss 60-61).

The First World War started as an enlarged version of older European wars with some residue of the older gentlemanly style, as evidenced by the informal Christmas truces of 1914 on the Western Front. By war's end, however, the full measure of total war had developed, and a good example of this is a proposal by the U.S. Army for a massive balloon campaign against Germany as a whole.

A balloon campaign may sound harmless, but this proposal was for 175,000 balloons that carried incendiary devices and poison gas canisters. The proposal was to an extent based on the experience of meteorological balloons. Through them it was known that between 10,000 and 15,000 feet, the winds over France blew primarily in the direction of Germany. The program overcame a number of technical problems and developed an inexpensive balloon that could be used to carry and deliver incendiary devices, poison gas canisters, or propaganda. The U.S. Army chemical warfare laboratory (at American University) developed a lightweight and reliable incendiary device, and the Army placed a large order with the main contractor, United Rubber Company. Ultimately, the program was preempted by the Armistice (Ziegler 761-762).

Airships and Balloons Before World War II

The peace treaty forced on Germany strongly limited German military activity. One clause in the document stipulated that Germany was forbidden to possess or develop airships, and that all airships were to be handed over. Some of the airships remained in German hands, and their crews burned them rather than hand them over (in a miniature version of the German High Seas Fleet scuttling itself at Scapa Flow after fleet had been interned by the British).

Following the defeat of Germany, many German military assets were awarded to different allied nations as war reparations, but the U.S. was not given a Zeppelin, so in 1922, the U.S. Navy contracted with Luftschiftbau Zeppelin of Freidrichshafen (in Southern Germany) for what would become the USS *Los Angeles*. The contract saved the German company from liquidation. Completed in 1924, the airship crossed the Atlantic, becoming the first airship from Germany crossing to the Americas. It was the longest-lasting airship commissioned in the Navy, in service from 1924-1939.

The Japanese were awarded a Zeppelin as reparations, the L-37, but after Japanese officers inspected the airship, they decided to ship only a few parts of it to Japan. There was some Japanese interest in airships, and several were constructed, but apparently there were continuing problems that did not justify the expenses, so the program was ended in 1932 (Starkings).

The USS *Los Angeles* was built to a commercial design. The lifting power came from internal ballonets and the internal structure was elaborate, and there were double bedrooms, a washroom, a sitting room and a galley, which seems to have provided excellent food. The flight to Lakehurst was by a German crew and used hydrogen, but upon arrival, the hydrogen was bled out and replaced with helium. Nine of the German officers and crew were contracted to train American crews how to operate the airship (Althoff 53-60).

The USS *Los Angeles*

The first American-built rigid airship was the USS *Shenandoah*. It was the first to use helium, and the first to cross the United States (Stockbridge 173), but the ship did not have the many amenities of the *Los Angeles*, and crews probably preferred being assigned to the latter ship.

Before World War I, helium had been discovered to exist in considerable quantities in a sample analysis from a Kansas gas well, coming in at 1.84% helium, but the discovery was ignored for years. Production was too small to be of any use in the war, but it increased after the war ended and a market for helium began to emerge. The U.S. Navy financed research into means of commercial extraction of the gas, and Congress enacted an embargo on helium in 1925 to preserve the resource and prioritize military use for the Navy (Levitt 10). Helium was, for many years, almost an American monopoly, although some helium also came from Canadian gas wells. Helium lofted the very large American airship fleet and some allied airships during World War II (American Chemical Society).

The Navy was quite interested in long-range scouting ahead of battle fleets. In 1919, the future utility of the aircraft carrier, including scouting aircraft, was not yet evident, so the Navy built facilities sufficient to test airship utility. At the Lakehurst site, they built an airship hangar that was for years the largest building in the world at 943 feet long. 350 feet wide and 200 feet high. The Lakehurst base originally had a hydrogen generating facility capable of generating 75,000 cubic feet of the gas per day, with gas storage. Helium was more expensive, at $120 per thousand cubic feet, but safety plus lowering helium costs won the Navy over. Among the other features for airships was a mooring mast 165 feet high (Althoff 13-15).

Helium proved its worth in 1925 with the USS *Shenandoah* disaster. The airship split in two, with half rising to 10,000 feet and then slowly coming down to the ground with many survivors. Only 29 of the 43 people on board survived, but had the ship been lifted by hydrogen, there likely would have been no survivors (Althoff 49).

A picture of the *Shenandoah* under construction at Lakehurst

A picture of the wreck

After the war, the U.S. Army contracted for a large airship in Italy, the *Roma,* to be used in some experiments and for training. In 1922, the ship hit a high-tension line near Langley Field, and its 1.2 million cubic feet of hydrogen produced a disaster, killing 34 of the 45 people aboard (Smith 115). This led to the exclusive use of non-flammable helium on American airships.

In December 1924, First Lieutenant Frank McGee "landed" his aircraft on a trapeze-shaped gear suspended from the blimp TC-3, which proved the ability of airships to carry airplanes. This was an Army project, and it faded away, apparently through lack of interest. The Army still had a few blimps at that time, but the Navy was given exclusive responsibility for rigid airships by 1920 (Smith 116).

During the 1930s, there was considerable interest in the possibility of carrying and launching aircrafts from airships. The Germans briefly dabbled with the idea of airships carrying an Albatross D-III fighter (an excellent fighter aircraft in its day) as a kind of built-in fighter escort to defend the airship, and the British experimented with launching a Sopwith Camel (another fine aircraft) from the airship R 23, with the idea of extending the fighter's range rather than defending the airship. Unlike the American concept, neither the British nor German concepts considered returning to the plane to the airship after it was launched (Smith 115).

The Navy was interested in the capabilities of large rigid airships, and in 1928 the Navy awarded a contract for two airships to the Goodyear-Zeppelin Corporation in Akron, Ohio. In 1931 and 1933, the USS *Akron* and the USS *Macon* were delivered.

Photo # NH 80773   F9C-2 in USS Akron's hangar, 1932

A Sparrowhawk plane in the *Akron*'s hangar

Prior to their delivery, the Navy continued experiments with airplanes and airships. In 1929, a Vought observation aircraft "landed" on the USS *Los Angeles*, and in 1931, airplanes again were landed on airships, using Consolidated N2Y training aircraft and landing at night. The *Akron* made its first flight in September 1931, but it did not receive its complement of pilots and its 6 Curtiss F9C-2 Sparrowhawk fighters until September 1932. Both the *Akron* and the *Macon* were designed as scouts for the fleet, had a very wide scouting radius, and an endurance of 5-6 days.

Airships had about a 40-mile visual range, so they could scout a path 80 miles wide. The aircraft doubled the sweep path to 160 miles and could also scout well ahead of the airship as a picket, in an era before radar was developed. The idea was sound, but there was an unanticipated problem in that airship crew and fleet personnel did not mesh well. The airship officers and the fighter pilots were viewed with contempt as brash (Smith 117).

In April 1933, the *Akron* was destroyed in a storm off the New Jersey coast, but the *Macon* made its initial flight in April 1933 and was based in Moffett Field in California. The airship performed in several fleet maneuvers in both the Pacific and the Caribbean, and was lost in 1935 (Smith 118, 120). Ultimately, the Navy concluded the airships were useless, as the Curtiss airplane on the airship was the world's smallest fighter, with no room in the cockpit for maps, charts or gadgets.

In 1937, the U.S. Bureau of Aeronautics explored a design for a ZRCV (Naval enthusiasts will recognize the CV designation as referring to an aircraft carrier). The design would accommodate 9 dive bombers (Smith 115).

The ZCRV would have been huge, at 892 feet long with more than 9 million cubic feet of helium capacity. The cruising speed would have been 50 knots and have a range of 4,300 miles and an endurance of a week. This compared well to a regular aircraft carrier in several respects, but the problem was lifting capacity - the ZCRV would have to carry pilots, airplanes, airplane fuel, armaments, and regular crew, and the craft's 297,000 pound carrying capacity was simply not enough. The aircraft would have been housed internally, each on its own trapeze, and fast developments in naval aircraft made the aircraft larger and larger. The Sparrowhawk fighters weighed in at 2,770 pounds, but the 1942 Grumman F4F, the standard Navy fighter, weighed 7,000 pounds.

Cost was also a factor. The SRCV was estimated at $10 million, and the standard PBY-1 flying boat cost $100,000. If one airship cost 100 flying boats, the arithmetic doomed the concept (Smith 120-121).

Airships between the wars were not all focused on the military. Germany went through a hideous economic period in the early 1920s and again in the Great Depression. Nonetheless, there was enough venture capital to fund some exploration of using airships for passenger service. In 1928, the Germans launched the *Graf Zeppelin*, which may be the most traveled airship in history.

The prewar airship airline DELAG resumed operations in the 1920s, after its two airships had been confiscated by the Allied Powers, and DELAG ran most German passenger airship operations until 1935, when it was replaced by a new, government-affiliated entity. Its most famous ship was the *Graf Zeppelin*, named for the inventor of Zeppelins. The *Graf Zeppelin* made its first trip across the Atlantic to Lakehurst in October 1928. It established that airship travel was reliable and a viable alternative to ocean travel. The ship visited Italy, Spain, and Palestine, and made 136 Atlantic crossings in all, which will probably remain a record.

In 1929, the *Graf Zeppelin* made a trip around the world, with the major sponsor being the American newspaper magnate William Randolph Hearst. Hearst insisted that the voyage start at Lakehurst, and he assigned a Hearst news reporter, a woman with the resounding name of Grace Marguerite Hay Drummond-Hay, who thus became the first woman to circumnavigate the globe by air. The route was Lakehurst to Friedrichshafen (the airship's base), Berlin, across Russia and Siberia to Tokyo, and then a long segment over the Pacific to Los Angeles. The last leg to Lakehurst was via El Paso, Kansas City, Chicago and Detroit. The trip lasted 21 days and covered 30,000 miles. Lady Hay Drummond-Hay filed reports for her newspaper whenever possible.

Lady Hay Drummond-Hay aboard the *Graf Zeppelin*

The *Graf Zeppelin*

The *Graf Zeppelin* was regularly used on flights to Recife and Rio in Brazil, as well as to New York. The very top of the Empire State Building has a mooring mast for an airship, but it was never used, and the Zeppelins landed at Lakehurst.

The Germans decided to build a second airship, the *Hindenburg,* named after Paul von *Hindenburg*, once German president and a towering figure in World War 1. This Zeppelin was carefully designed, and the intent was to compete with the transatlantic ocean liners, at that time the height of luxury travel. The Zeppelin could not offer the same level of luxury, but it did well enough, and was far faster than the liners. The ship was designed for helium, but the U.S. refused to provide any.

The *Hindenburg* had a dining and lounge area with specially designed lightweight aluminum chairs. The public rooms featured wall paintings by the artist Otto Arpke, painted by an unusual spray process on the airship fabric that lined the interior walls. Dinner service and silverware was specially crafted for the airship. Food appears to have been rather good, although a galley in an airship filled with hydrogen seems inherently risky.

The Zeppelin worked well over the North Atlantic in summer season, with flights to North America, and over the South Atlantic in the winter season to Brazil. Fares to the United States were 1,000 to 1,200 marks, and 1,500 to Brazil. Passenger cabins were quite small, 78 inches by 66 inches, with one bunk fixed and another that could be pulled down from the wall. These were much smaller than rooms on a liner, but they were equivalent to overnight accommodations on railways. The Zeppelin could cruise at about 80-85 miles an hour for fuel economy, well below top speed, but several times faster than ocean liners (Zeppelin Museum). Both airships carried passengers across the Atlantic, and they provided status for the rising Nazi Party, with both having swastikas.

The *Hindenburg* in 1936

Today, of course, the *Hindenburg* is known for its tragic fate. On the night of May 6, 1937, the *Hindenburg* arrived at Lakehurst by 7:00 but was unable to land because the ground crew needed to haul her down was not yet in place. By this time, many of the passengers were anxiously peering out the windows, hoping to soon be returned to terra firma, and at 7:11, Captain Pruss began applying the brakes and trying to stop the zeppelin over the landing target. However, he was unable to keep the ship steady in the crosswinds, so he had to make another pass over the field. As he did so, he ordered some of the water used as ballast to be dumped so that the stern would be lighter. Those standing on the field to watch the zeppelin land began to pull out their raincoats and umbrellas as a light drizzle began to fall. Some would later claim that it looked like gas was leaking from an upper fin, but that was never verified.

Finally, at 7:21, Pruss ordered the mooring lines dropped. Mather watched with interest as the ground crew picked up the ropes and began tying them to the mooring tackled on the ground, and Belin continued chatting with her as Mrs. Pannes slipped away to get her coat. Meanwhile, the Doehner family and other passengers were watching the landing maneuvers from the dining room windows. Mr. Doehner was filming the action and left his family to go back to their stateroom for another roll of film. The boys were talking and asking questions of a steward, Severin Klein, who was doing his best to keep up with their prattle.

Meanwhile, on the ground, Herbert Morrison was broadcasting the ship's landing live on the radio: "The ship was riding majestically toward us like some great feather. Riding as though it was mighty proud of the place it was playing in the world's aviation. The ship is no doubt bustling with activity as we can see. Orders were shouted to the crew, the passengers are probably lining the windows looking down at the field ahead of them, getting their glimpse of the mooring mast. And these giant flagships standing here, the American airline flagships waiting to rush them to all points in the United States when they get the ship moored. There are a number of important personages on board and no doubt the new commander, Captain Max Pruss, is thrilled too for this, his great moment, the first time he's commanded the *Hindenburg*. On previous nights he acted as chief officer under Captain Lehmann."

It was 7:25 when a blue flash caught some of the people's eyes. It may have been an optical illusion or static electricity or perhaps even the nearly mythical St. Elmo's Fire, but whatever it was, it was quickly forgotten as fire broke out from that region and began to spread across the hull of the ship. Morrison was continuing his broadcast as the mooring ropes were secured and was still talking as the *Hindenburg* caught fire: "It's practically standing still now, they've dropped ropes out of the nose of the ship and it's been taken ahold of down on the field by a number of men. It's starting to rain again, the rain had slacked up a little bit... the back motors of the ship are just holding it, just enough to keep it from... It's burst into flames!"

Though an experienced newscaster, even Morrison began to lose his composure, alternating between broadcasting and crying out to those in harm's way: "Get this, Charlie; get this, Charlie! It's fire... and it's crashing! It's crashing terrible! Oh, my! Get out of the way, please! It's burning and bursting into flames and the... and it's falling on the mooring mast. And all the folks agree that this is terrible; this is the worst of the worst catastrophes in the world…its flames... Crashing, oh! Four- or five-hundred feet into the sky and it... it's a terrific crash, ladies and gentlemen. It's smoke, and it's in flames now; and the frame is crashing to the ground, not quite to the mooring mast. Oh, the humanity! And all the passengers screaming around here. I told you; it—I can't even talk to people, their friends are on there! Ah! It's... it... it's a... ah! I... I can't talk, ladies and gentlemen. Honest: it's just laying there, mass of smoking wreckage. Ah! And everybody can hardly breathe and talk and the screaming. I...I...I'm sorry. Honest: I... I can hardly breathe. I... I'm going to step inside, where I cannot see it. Charlie, that's terrible. Ah, ah... I can't. Listen, folks; I...I'm gonna have to stop for a minute because I've lost my voice. This is the worst thing I've ever witnessed."

Looking back on the seconds that it took for the *Hindenburg* to be completely engulfed, it later became clear that, for most people, location was destiny. Those in the nose of the ship were killed instantly or so badly burned that they lived for only a few hours, and the same was true for those who were in the staterooms or the lower part of the ship. While most of those in other parts of the ship survived, something as simple as one's position in a certain room often determined one's level of injury.

Of those who survived, few had as horrific a tale to tell as Philip Mangone: "Somehow, in the flashing second of the explosion, I retained my presence of mind. I grabbed a chair and smashed it through the window. I gripped the window sill and looked out. We seemed a little less than 200 feet high. I said to myself, 'I can't jump. We're too high. I'll break my legs.' But I couldn't wait. A moment or two later, as the wrecked ship sank downward, I jumped. The framework of the dirigible pinned me down. I lay flat in the tangle of wreckage, but my body wasn't crushed. I worked frantically to get myself out of the wreckage. Desperately, I scraped a hole into the dirt. Somehow I burrowed myself out like a mole. I was conscious all the time. It seemed like an age before I squirmed through. I stood up, dazed. I wheeled around dizzily. The shock had been so great I didn't know what I was doing. I was navigating without thinking. All around me was the smell of burning flesh. Men were rushing about excitedly. Some were badly burned passengers, others members of the ground crew. The scene was indescribable. Everything was in a panic. Passengers were crying and screaming. I reeled under my own steam toward a building in the distance." Mangone later added, "I was 'alive' for several hours. That is, I knew what I was doing. The burns hadn't got to me yet; I didn't feel them too much. But that night, in the hospital, I was knocked out. I lapsed into unconsciousness. I was in great pain just before my sense deserted me. I was unconscious for a week and after that I was sick for weeks."

Within 60 seconds of the first explosion, the *Hindenburg* was on the ground and engulfed in flames. Those that would survive the disaster were out, while most of those who would not were already dead. Of the 36 people who died that day, most were lucky enough to be gone almost instantly, killed by the explosion itself. However, those who survived to make it to the hospitals faced slow, agonizing deaths that were most likely hastened by the amount of morphine they were given for their pain. Even 21st century medicine is often impotent in the face of serious burns, and even less care was available in 1937.

Within five minutes, all those who would survive were out of the burning rubble and were either receiving medical attention or wondering around looking for their loves ones. Around the same time, Morrison returned to the air with information for those desperately hoping for some good news. Having gained his composure, he announced, "Well, ladies and gentlemen, I'm back again. I raced down to the burning ship, and just as I walked up to the ship, over climbed those picket lines, I met a man coming out… dazed… dazed, he couldn't find his way. I grabbed ahold of him: it's Philip Mangone. Philip Mangone, M-A-N-G-O-N-E, of New York. Philip Mangone… he's burned terribly in the hands, and he's burned terribly in the face, his eyebrows and… all his hair is burned off, but he's walking and talking, plainly and distinctly, and he told me he jumped! He jumped with other passengers! Now, there's a Mr. Spay, it sounds like Spay, we're not sure of it, and, uh, he also got out, and we noticed the, uh, lines…the different lines, the, uh, airship lines, and the American Airways, their ambulances are down there, and they're taking people out of the wreckage! It seems that a number of them jumped clear when the explosion occurred in the tail. Now, I – I've just been running up with Mr. Mangone, and put him in a car, his wife and daughter met him, and I put them in the car with him, and sent him to the field hospital with the other passengers who have been saved."

Had the *Hindenburg* burned 10-15 years earlier, chances are that there might have been a more thorough investigation of the cause of the explosion. That is not to say that those looking into the matter did not give it their full attention, but there was so much distrust between the United States, where the incident occurred, and Germany, the ship's home port, that both parties were likely more interested in figuring out how to blame the other for the incident than in finding out the truth. To many Americans, it seemed that the Germans nefariously planned for the

Hindenburg to burst into flames on American soil, while many Germans believed that the ship, the pride of the Hinterland, must have been sabotaged by the jealous Americans.

For his part, Captain Pruss maintained to his dying day that his airship must have been the victim of some sort of evil plot, in part because believing otherwise could have called his decisions into question. The company that would have to bear the liability for any loss felt likewise. Those who constructed the *Hindenburg* and her sisters insisted that only sabotage or human error could be responsible for what happened, since they did not want to shoulder any blame for themselves.

According to a report made by the American Secretary of Commerce about his investigation, there was no evidence of foul play: "After carefully weighing the oral evidence and transcribing to a master diagram the numerous diagrams on which the ground witnesses indicated their first observations of fire, we conclude that the first open flame, produced by the burning of the ship's hydrogen, appeared on the top of the ship forward of the entering edge of the vertical fin over Cells 4 and 5. The first open flame that was seen at that place was followed after a very brief interval by a burst of flaming hydrogen between the equator and the top of the ship. The fire spread in all directions moving progressively forward at high velocity with a succession of mild explosions. As the stern quarter became enveloped, the ship lost buoyancy and cracked at about one-quarter of the distance from the rear end. The forward part assumed a bow-up attitude, the rear appearing to remain level. At the same time the ship was settling to the ground at a moderate rate of descent. Whereas there was a definite detonation after flame was first observed on the ship, we believe that the phenomenon was initially a rapid burning or combustion — not an explosion. From the observations made, it appears that there was a quantity of free hydrogen present in the after part of the ship when the fire originated."

It was that free hydrogen described in the report that would be the smoking gun in the investigation. If there was indeed a leak, and if that leak was purely accidental, then there was less reason to believe that any type of sabotage took place. Of course, the leak could have been manmade, but it would have been difficult for anyone to reach that portion of the ship. Furthermore, the leak itself would have posed no problem had a spark not come along to ignite it.

In the end, it fell to the German High Command to issue a ruling on the cause of the explosion. Put simply, their conclusion was that no conclusion could be drawn: "In spite of thorough questioning of all the witnesses, in spite of a thorough-going inspection and search of the wreckage, and in spite of evaluation of all pictorial documents giving testimony of the sequence of the fire, no completely certain proof can be found for any of the possibilities cited above. In view of the fact that in the German Zeppelin airship traffic in an operation period of decades no accidents have occurred while utilizing hydrogen as lifting gas, and on the basis of all testimony of witnesses and investigations, the commission has gained the conviction, that everything had been done by all parties responsible for the frictionless execution of the airship traffic to forestall an accident. If therefore not any one of the previously-mentioned possibilities of criminal attack can be considered, the Commission can only assume as a cause of the airship fire a cooperation of a number of unfortunate circumstances in a case of force majeure." The committee went on to conclude that the only accidental cause for the explosion was a combination of a leaking hydrogen cell and a spark caused by either by some sort of mild lightning or static electricity.

No matter the actual cause, the *Hindenburg* disaster quickly spelled the end of passengers traveling across the Atlantic on zeppelins, despite the fact that such airships had logged more than a million miles safely. At the same time, the fact that technological advances in airplanes made it possible to fly much faster may have made the decline or zeppelins inevitable anyway. Whether the zeppelins would've faded into obscurity with or without the disaster is a question, but some people were still able to put the *Hindenburg* and its untimely demise into perspective. In showing video footage of the disaster, Britain's Pathe newsreel concluded with these remarks: "The *Hindenburg* has gone. She represented man's latest attempt to conquer the Atlantic by air. Her tragedy will not halt the march of progress. From her ashes will arise the knowledge, from her fate the lesson, that will lead to a greater and a better means of mastering the air. If so, her dead will not have died in vain."

Picture of a memorial marker commemorating the site of the *Hindenburg* disaster

All the while, people were still tinkering with balloons, and the late 1920s and early 1930s brought the advent of stratospheric ballooning. This was both a pursuit after altitude records and scientific investigation of what the atmosphere was like that high up. In 1927, Captain Hawthorne Gray of the U.S. Army Air Corps made three ascents (the Air Force did not become a separate service until after the war). In his first flight, he reached 29,000 feet, and on his second flight he reached 42,000 feet, but it was not accepted as a record because the balloon malfunctioned and he had to parachute. On his third flight in 1927, he reached 42,000 feet in an open basket gondola. When the balloon reached ground, the officer was found dead, due to the lack of oxygen and the thin atmosphere.

A picture of Gray before his fateful flight

Auguste Picard was a Swiss inventor, scientist and adventurer who realized that a pressurized capsule would be required for aeronauts to survive at the altitudes being reached. He built a spherical gondola, sealed and pressurized, to be suspended below the balloon. In 1932, he and Paul Kepfer reached an altitude of 51,000 feet, and in 1933, Picard and a passenger reached 53,000 feet. Also in 1933, an American in the balloon *Century of Progress* reached 61,000 feet. In 1934, a Soviet balloon crew reached about 72,000 feet, but it killed them.

The record was achieved in 1935, when two U.S. Army Air Corps officers in a helium balloon reached above 72,000 feet, a record that stood for 21 years. After that point, the interest in flying up into the stratosphere lessened and no more such flights were attempted until after World War II.

Airships and Balloons in World War II

In the wake of Pearl Harbor, the U.S. Navy had 10 airships, and only 4 were militarily useful: the K class ships. Several were airships inherited from the Army, which had abandoned airship development in 1937, and the U.S. was the only combatant to operate airships during the war.

The American airships used in the war varied considerably; the L ships were used for training, and several of these were former Goodyear advertising blimps. The workhorse of the airship fleet was the K ship class, 135 of which were built during the war. They were used for patrol and for convoy escort duties. The K ships were 253 feet long and 60 feet in diameter, with 456,000 cubic feet of helium capacity. They were powered with two large Pratt and Whitney engines and could stay aloft for 60 hours. Their armament for anti-submarine patrols was four depth charges and a .50 caliber machine gun, which was sufficient to sink a submarine (Levitt 11).

It took some time for the main contractor, the Goodyear Corporation, to ramp up production. By the end of 1942, Goodyear delivered 26 airships, but in the first half of 1943, Goodyear and other contractors delivered 48 airships, and in the second half of the year they delivered 55 more (Levitt 15). That level of production was phenomenal, and yet another indication of the overwhelming industrial capacity of the United States.

There were some early problems, one of which is a mystery. The L-8 took off on August 8, 1942 from Moffett Field (near San Jose, California), and a few hours later, the ship drifted in. However, the ship came back with the two crew members missing, and they were never found. Earlier that year, the G-1 and the L-2 collided off New Jersey, with 12 lives lost. The G-1 was flying without any kind of light (Levitt 13).

A picture of the L-8

The only combat between a U.S. airship and a German submarine (the U-134) took place on July 18, 1943. The K-74, a U.S. blimp out of Richmond Naval Air Station near Miami, was on a night patrol, and the conditions were optimal for spotting surfaced submarines, with a nearly full moon and good visibility. The airship was traveling at 500 feet and 47 knots, and at 2340 hours, radar indicated a submarine (Levitt 15). Navy policy was for an airship to stand off, keep the enemy in view, and summon help, but the pilot decided to attack, at 250 feet altitude and at 53 knots. The dirigible was armed with depth charges and a .50 caliber machine gun. The depth charges were dropped, but the crew forgot to arm them. The U-boat's deck guns shot down the airship, which would have been a very large target directly overhead and hard to miss, and the Germans boarded the wreckage of the shot-down dirigible and took photographs. One crew member was lost to shark attack, but the rest of the crew was rescued (Levitt 15-16).

The U-boat later rendezvoused with another submarine and passed on the photographs. U-134 was spotted and attacked by British anti-submarine aircraft and was sunk with all hands near Spain.

One little-known task that blimps proved to be outstanding for was spotting mines. Working in conjunction with minesweepers, they made the extremely hazardous activities of minesweeping less dangerous and more effective. It became the custom to have an experienced officer on board the airship as liaison between airship and vessel (Levitt 16).

The U.S. Navy eventually possessed the largest fleet of airships ever assembled, and the blimps' overall impact on repressing U-boat activity can't be quantified. The convoy system, an ever-larger number of escort vessels such as frigates and destroyers, the development of escort carriers (small aircraft carriers) and vastly improved radar and sonar, all combined to win the Battle of the Atlantic. It seems probable that the loss of so many experienced U-boat crews also affected the campaign, but what airships did do well was facilitate the rescue of hundreds of sailors. In 1942 the airships flew more than 2,600 operational missions, more than 17,000 in 1943, and more than 27,000 in 1944 (Levitt 15).

Airships were far less used in the Pacific, although they patrolled the West Coast, with their primary base being at Moffett Field near San Francisco. Japanese submarines were every bit as good as the German boats, but Japanese naval doctrine used submarines to attack enemy naval vessels, not transport convoys.

In 1944, the U.S. Navy decided to send a squadron of blimps to North Africa. The process of getting them to the Mediterranean resulted in the first crossing of the Atlantic by non-rigid airships, from the U.S. to Bermuda, and on to the Azores. Once there, they proved useful in monitoring the Strait of Gibraltar for U-boats, because their slower speed and greater endurance worked better than the PBY aircraft previously used (Levitt 16). U-boats sometimes managed to sneak through into the Mediterranean, but blimps and other measures made it a highly dangerous place for German submarines.

In the end, the highly influential Naval historian Samuel Eliot Morison evaluated blimps as ineffective, simply because a submarine could spot them miles away. That comment seems equivocal, because a submarine that saw an airship escort miles away would likely quickly submerge for fear of being spotted.

Military technology during the war became deadlier and more complex. Balloons were no longer needed for observation of the enemy and were no longer used for artillery spotting, but they still did important work. One balloon tool was very simple: the barrage balloon. Barrage balloons essentially lifted a tough steel cable that could damage or down low altitude attacks by enemy airplanes. An airplane that collided with a cable could lose a wing and crash. Barrage balloons, a cheap and effective option, interfered with low altitude attacks such as strafing, mine laying, or torpedo launches.

Barrage balloons, posted along the Thames estuary near London, interfered with German mine-laying aircraft. In August 1940, the Germans attempted to destroy that balloon barrier, destroying about 40 of the balloons but losing six aircraft in the process. Balloons also protected beachheads in North Africa and in Italy from low-flying German aircraft. During the 1944 German V-1 rocket campaign, against London, barrage balloons were deployed to help protect the city. The V-1 was not very accurate, and the rockets were simply aimed in the general direction of London, but the rockets still managed to inflict considerable damage and casualties. Anti-aircraft guns downed 1,878 of the slow flying rockets, and Allied fighters destroyed 1,846. The balloons downed 231 of these early cruise missiles.

In all, the British deployed about 2,000 barrage balloons during the war, forming 52 balloon companies involving about 33,000 service personnel. Americans initially deployed far fewer, and at first only had a few hundred on the West Coast to defend Pacific ports. The U.S. deployed three barrage balloon batteries, each with 45 balloons, to defend ports in North Africa and Italy.

During World War II, the U.S. operated 15 squadrons of blimps, about 200 in all. These escorted a total of some 89,000 ships in convoys, and accounted for some 550,000 flight hours. Not a single ship was lost to enemy action in the convoys escorted by blimps (Stepler i).

The main balloon project in the Pacific was a Japanese balloon campaign directed against the United States. It resembled in some ways the aborted Austrian balloon attack on Venice in 1849, and the planned attack on Germany by the Americans in 1918 that was made redundant by the Armistice. From late 1944-April 1945, the Japanese launched about 9,000 balloons against the United States, with prevailing westerly winds blowing them to the Pacific Northwest. Each balloon carried a 33-pound incendiary bomb, and about a thousand of the balloons made it.

This balloon attack was the only Japanese offensive against the mainland United States, and it caused the only American civilian casualties on the mainland. A family found one, tried to figure out what it was, and the bomb burst and killed six people. Nothing about the balloons appeared in the American press, so as not to let the Japanese know that any balloons had actually reached the target. The last one was found in Alaska in 1955, still lethal.

Airships and Balloons after World War II

In 1952, the U.S. began a program called Flying Cloud to develop balloon bombers. The concept was balloon "bombers" that could drift over the Soviet Union to drop incendiary devices, lethal gas, and "newly developed biological poisons," which may refer to biological agents such as anthrax. The program was made redundant by the fast development of effective nuclear weapon delivery systems, such as guided missiles and improved bomber aircraft, so Flying Cloud was cancelled in 1955 (Ziegler 767).

The most familiar name in American airships is the famous Goodyear blimp. The Goodyear company operated commercial blimps from 1911-1958, and in that span, Goodyear carried 483,000 passengers on a total of 179,000 flights, with no injuries or fatalities (Stepler ii). The Goodyear Blimp persisted for decades and became one of the most recognized company symbols in advertising history. The Goodyear airships were used for such projects as providing panoramic television shots of packed college football stadiums and of large public events. Most of the Americans who have seen an actual airship have seen one of the Goodyear dirigibles.

Balloons can lift instruments to record weather conditions aloft, and to conduct atmospheric research. Weather balloons actually go back more than a century, to the beginnings of scientific meteorology in the late 1800s. The U.S. Army proposal at the end of World War 1 to unleash thousands of balloon bombs on Germany was rooted in the weather balloon service. Experience with weather balloons gave the planners of that project the knowledge of wind currents and the experience with balloon technology that made the project more than theoretical.

Weather balloons are probably, by at least one level of magnitude, the most common category of balloons. Modern weather balloons carry a reporting device called a radiosonde, which reports on atmospheric conditions. The balloons are about 6 feet in diameter, but they expand to 20 or more feet in diameter at high altitudes, where they burst. They can carry the radiosondes to an astonishing 100,000 feet.

Weather balloons are launched twice daily at 600 sites around the world. American radiosondes are equipped with a parachute and include a mailing bag with instructions on how to return them to the National Weather Service. Through that process, about 20% of the 75,000 radiosondes used in the U.S. each year are recovered. The atmospheric data provided by the balloon-carried radiosondes is what makes accurate weather predictions possible. In a sense, the use of balloons is an important aspect of all aviation and transportation generally, due to the way commercial aviation relies on accurate weather projections (National Weather Service).

In 1955, the U.S. Navy explored the notion of using the old method of hot air for floating balloons because helium gas was costly and hydrogen remained dangerous. The Navy contracted with Raven Industries to develop a practical hot air balloon, which came into being in 1963. By then, however, the Navy had phased out balloons, and the Raven design was no longer needed. When the possibilities of manufacturing the balloons for the Navy dried up, the Raven Company began marketing the design as a sporting balloon, and the popularity of the design literally took off (Godfrey 228).

The Navy never completely lost interest in balloons and airships. In 2006, the U.S. Navy acquired its first non-rigid airship since 1962, a demonstration ship, the MZ-3A. It proved to be useful in the Deepwater Horizon oil spill disaster of 2010, but otherwise seems to have been of little interest (Althoff 267).

Balloons continued to be popular as children's toy and for celebrations. A movie by Pixar, titled *Up!*, featured a small house carried far up and away by a huge and colorful mass of balloons. What is less known, however, is that there was a real parallel to the movie that did not end so happily. On April 20, 2008, Father Adelir Arturo de Carli launched from Paranagua in Brazil. He took off in a buoyancy chair, a satellite phone, thermal flying suit and a GPS device, lifted by a thousand small helium balloons. Photographs show a colorful mass of balloons rising up with him and his equipment dangling below.

Father de Carli, or Padre Baloniero as his parishioners called him, had made such a flight before, a 4-hour flight using 600 helium filled party balloons. His idea for this flight was to raise funds for a charity, and on the way up he had a phone interview with the Brazilian network, Globo. He reached 19,000 feet before vanishing, and months later his remains were found at sea. There are stories that some of his parishioners expect Padre Baloniero to return as a saint, in a whirl of balloons (Holmes 3-4).

In Europe, particularly Germany, there is renewed interest in airships. A design called the Zeppelin NT has been designed and built by Zeppelin Luftschifftechnik GmbH. It has been described as a very innovative semi-rigid design, and is now being used in Germany in the tourism industry (Althoff 267).

Recent American uses of aerostats have included Tethered Aerostat Radar Systems (TARS) used for surveillance along the border and in the Caribbean, for drug war interventions. These aerostats could lift 2,200 pounds to 12,000 feet, detect targets to 230 miles, and have a prolonged endurance. The U.S. deployed smaller aerostats to Kosovo and Afghanistan, called Rapidly Elevated Aerostat Platform (REAP). These operated about 300 feet above the battlefield, carrying both daylight and night vision cameras (Bolkcom 2).

The U.S. Army has also deployed a Rapid Aerostat Initial Development (RAID) program, which were twice the size of REAP, operating at about 1,000 feet, and carrying a suite of day and night-vision cameras. Proposals have been made and canceled with the vagaries of Congressional appropriations. One such had the intriguing name of Project Walrus, for a hybrid airship that could transport 1,000 tons over international distances, which was canceled in 2006 (Bolkcom 3).

Airships are both an old-fashion technology and one with considerable potential for the future. Helium still can lift airships and balloons, and the craft have more endurance in the air, unlike aircrafts that require refueling. Even the biggest passenger jets don't have a 24-hour endurance, while airships can stay aloft for a week or more. Airships do require fuel, but much less than fixed-wing aircraft.

Recreational ballooning has also become significant. Starting in the 1960s, the number of hobbyists has quite literally ballooned. There are a wide variety of balloon events, both for hot air and for gas balloons, along with contests in a variety of categories, and annual balloon fests that attract substantial tourist attention in cities like Albuquerque, New Mexico, where the city's altitude gives balloonists more than a mile's height without being off the ground. It's not clear how many balloons are in use in the United States; the Federal Aviation Agency's annual aviation survey showed 2,945 lighter than air aircraft in the country in 2017. There are a few FAA regulations, but recreational ballooning is not as regulated as other segments of American aviation.

The Balloon Federation of America may be the biggest recreational ballooning organization in the United States. The BFA has divisions for hot air and gas balloons, and maintains a National Balloon Museum in Indianola, Iowa. It conducts national competitive events in a number of classes, both for men and for women, along with conducting classes. It also has a Professional Rides Operators division that requires commitment to a code of acceptable safety and business procedures (BFA).

While the recreation as a whole has an excellent reputation for safety, the old parameters still apply. Any flight above 10,000 feet requires care and training in oxygen equipment and knowledge about appropriate clothing because of the variance in temperature at altitude. Hydrogen remains explosive, and balloons remain affected by wind and weather, although today's balloons are robustly constructed of materials the Mongolfier brothers could never have imagined back in the 18th century.

Helium remains largely an American monopoly. The gas has a number of uses, such as pressurization of liquid propellants, superconductivity research, and has proven to be useful in wind tunnels. The U.S. Bureau of Land Management manages the helium reserves, including leasing and storage (American Chemical Society). Helium is a diminishing resource, but it is still used for millions of children's birthday parties and for all kinds of celebrations.

One possibility is using airships as heavy lift vehicles (HLV). There are current designs for large airships with a lifting power of 1,000 tons that could carry and deliver goods much more cheaply than regular aircraft and be competitive with trucks and rails, although less so than shipping by sea. They could also deliver heavy cargo in places without massive infrastructure. They might work very well for deliveries to remote settlements, or energy development complexes otherwise not easy to reach.

There may also be some military use for high altitude airships (HAA), although the most efficient altitude for airship operation is under 15,000 feet (Stockbridge 174-175). A special problem for these is that the atmosphere is so thin, so helium has limited lifting power. A significant payload would take a large airship (Balkcom 3).

HAA craft would offer some advantages. Serving at altitudes above 60,000 feet, they would be out of the range of most antiaircraft artillery fire or surface to air missiles. They can be designed to be very difficult to detect by radar, acoustic or thermal reflection, and they are good platforms for intelligence, surveillance, and reconnaissance.

Airships may be particularly useful in areas where there is no air defense system to contend with, as in Afghanistan. They could be useful weapons platforms, perhaps more economical than drones. Airship endurance is a strong plus, and they don't need a pilot so if one were in fact downed, it would avoid the political complexities of a captured pilot.

There are new-era Zeppelins referred to as Zeppelins NT that are far smaller than the old Zeppelins and are used mostly for short tourist flights in Germany. They were first built in the early 1990s. The interior structure uses carbon fiber crossbeams linked to three aluminum girders, reinforced by bracing cables. The 298,000 cubic feet of gas is contained in ballonets, and the structure is strong and extremely light. If the ghost of Count Zeppelin ever lurked around Friedrichshafen, surely he'd approve.

An unusual problem with airships is that so few people are trained in how to fly them. There are thought to be about 130 people in the U.S. who are sufficiently trained to operate an airship.

HybridAir, an aviation company in Britain has tested a quite novel bi-hulled design it calls the Airlander 10, which underwent several test flights in 2018. The airship is multipurpose, with passenger and cargo configurations. The company appears to be appealing to a luxury clientele that might be interested in three-day excursions, and the accommodations go back to the *Hindenburg* days, with lounge space and rather elegant style. The sleeping rooms are larger than those tiny sleeping rooms on the 1930s Zeppelin.

The Airlander 10 will have a 5-day airborne endurance, a 4,000 mile range, and will be capable of an altitude of 20,000 feet. The luxury passenger configuration can take up to 19 passengers; and the commercial payload will be about 10 tons. The airships should be operational in the early 2020s.

Balloons are rarely thought of as spacecraft, yet in the U.S., NASA has been using balloons in atmospheric and near-space research for almost 40 years, and there are plans for using balloons to explore other worlds. NASA has launched about 1,700 balloons over a 35-year period from a number of different locations around the world. The NASA balloons serve a wide variety of purposes. One is to carry student experiments high in the atmosphere and encourage students to choose careers in science and space fields. Balloons are used to study the gas composition of the upper atmosphere, to measure cosmic rays and other radiation, measure electromagnetism, and even search for the intergalactic medium.

One kind of balloon that NASA regularly uses is ULDB (Ultra Long Distance Balloons), also known as super pressure balloons. The most commonly used size is 40 million cubic feet, large enough to fit 195 Goodyear blimps inside, and the envelope if spread out would cover 20 acres. That makes these balloons among the largest ever launched. Missions may last 100 days and the balloons float up to 120,000 feet, in the near-fringes of space.

The other main type is the zero-pressure balloon, which is open at the bottom. The zero-pressure balloons have much shorter flight durations at two or three days. The balloons use helium. They are made from a thin plastic, about the same thickness as normal kitchen sandwich wrap (NASA).

In August of 2018, NASA launched the "Big 60," a 60 million cubic feet balloon, which reached 159,000 feet where it could sustain flight. The balloon is as big as a football field.

NASA has plans for planetary ballooning, literally using balloons on other planets. Balloons offer a platform with a more flexible range of action, more than a satellite orbiting the target world, and more than rovers crawling on the surface. Missions that may use balloons may go to Mars, Venus and Saturn's largest moon, Titan. Other worlds will have other atmospheres that differ from Earth's in density, composition, pressure and temperature, all things balloons can measure.

Online Resources

Other books about 19th century history by Charles River Editors

Other books about balloons and airships on Amazon

Bibliography

Allaz, Camille. *The History of Air Cargo and Airmail.* Manchester, UK: ChristopherFoyle Publishing, 2012. Published in association with the International Air Cargo Association. French edition published 1998.

Century of Flight, Org. "Civil War Balloons." www.century-of-flight-net/new%20site/balloons/ civil%20war.htm/ Accessed July 11, 2019.

Fischer, William E. "Into the Night: The Evolution of Flight Under Cover of Darkness Before the First World War." *Air Power History*, 40 (1), Spring 1993. 3-12.

Godfrey, Tim. "A Juvenile Lecture by Tim Godfrey." *Journal of the Royal Society of Arts*, #5212 (March 1974), 225-229. Accessed vis JSTOR, May 30, 2019.

Harding, Richard; Mills, F. John. Special Forms of Flight 1: Balloons, Gliders and Hang Gliders. *British Medical Journal,* 287 (23 July 1983). 277-278.

Hiam, C.Michael. *Dirigible Dreams: The Age of the Airship*. Dartmouth, NH: University Press of New England, 2014.

Holmes, Richard. *Falling Upward: How We Took to the Air*. London: William Collins, 2013.

Hopkins, Sara. "America's Champion Aeronaut in the Civil War: Daredevil Balloonist John. H. Steiner." *Military Images* 33 (4), Fall 2015. 42-45, Accessed via JSTOR, July 10, 2019.

Kuhn, Gary. "Fiestas and Fiascoes—Balloon Flights in Nineteenth Century Mexico." *Journal of Sport History* 13 (2), Summer 1986. 111-18. Accessed via JSTOR July 7, 2019.

Murphy, Justin O. *Military Aircraft, Origins to 1918, An Illustrated History of Their Impact*. ABC-CLIO. Santa Barbara, California, 2005.

National Balloon Museum. "History of Ballooning." https://nationalballoonmuseum.com/about/history-of-ballooning/ Accessed July 7, 2019.

Nilson, Peter, and Hartman, Steve. "Winged Man and Flying Ships: Medieval Flying Journals and Eternal Dreams of Flight." *Georgia Review*, 50 (2), Summer 1996. 267-292. Accessed via JSTOR, July 10, 2019.

Pearl, Jason. "Hot Air Balloons Are Useless." The Atlantic Online, Technology. July 15, 2018. https:/www.theatlantic.com/technology/archive/2018/07/hot-air-balloons-are-useless/565025/. Accessed July 7, 2019.

Scott, Major Joseph C. "The Infernal Balloon: Union Aeronautics During the Civil War." *Army History*, #93, Fall 2014. 6-27. Accessed via JSTOR, May 30, 2019.

Smith, Maurice H. "Travel by Air Before 1900." The Princeton University Library Chronicle 27 (3). Spring 1966. 143-55. Accessed via JSTOR July 7, 2019.

Stockbridge, Casey; Ceruti, Alessandro; and Marzocca, Pier. "Airship Research and Development in the Areas of Design, Structures, Dynamics and Energy Systems." *International Journal of Aeronautical and Space Science*, 13 (2), 2012. 170-187.

Strekfuss, James. *Eyes All Over the Sky*. Havertown, PA: Casemate 2016.

Ullman, Bruce. The War Balloon *Santiago*." *Aerospace Historian*, 32 (5) Summer 1985. 117-129. Accessed via JSTOR, July 10, 2019.

Van Eaton, Colonel Erroll H. "Airships and the Modern Military." U.S.Army War College. Carlisle Barracks, Pennsylvania, 1991.

Williams, James W. "A History of Army Aviation From Its Beginnings to the War on Terror." US Army Aviation Museum Foundation, Inc. iUniverse, Lincoln, Nebraska. Accessed June 20, 2019.

Ziegler, Charles A. "Weapons Development in Context: The Case of the World War 1 Balloon Bomber." *Technology and Culture*, 34 (4), October 1994. 750-767. Accessed via JSTOR, July10, 2019.

Free Books by Charles River Editors

We have brand new titles available for free most days of the week. To see which of our titles are currently free, click on this link.

Discounted Books by Charles River Editors

We have titles at a discount price of just 99 cents everyday. To see which of our titles are currently 99 cents, click on this link.

Made in the USA
Monee, IL
28 January 2020